SALADS
AND DRESSINGS

SALADS
AND DRESSINGS

16 Fish and seafood

42 Poultry and meat

66 Cheese

Contents

Introduction

Salads have undergone a remarkable resurgence in recent years. Once associated with limp lettuce and soggy tomatoes, they have cast off their reputation as "rabbit food," and are now recognized as delicious dishes in their own right.

The sheer variety of recipes in *Salads and Dressings* proves just how versatile and exciting the humble salad can be. Offering up more than 100 dishes, from Middle Eastern tabboulehs to traditional French classics, this book provides salad inspiration for every occasion. Light summer lunches stand alongside rustic winter warmers; traditional flavor pairings are complemented by foods and spices you may have never tried before.

All this doesn't mean that the recipes in this book are complex or time-consuming. On the contrary, *Salads and Dressings* comes complete with tips on creating instant salad meals using no-cook ingredients, as well as advice on turning almost any salad into an on-the-go packed lunch.

Since no salad is complete without a dressing, the last chapter in this book provides a handful of dedicated dressing recipes to inspire you, and also shows you how to mix up your own flavor pairings.

Instant or leisurely, simple or decadent, classic or contemporary—a salad can suit any occasion.

Instant salads

When time is short, salads can be the perfect mealtime choice. Stock up on a selection of raw and precooked foods, and you'll be able to throw together a nutritious meal in minutes.

Using raw foods

Quick to prepare and serve, raw salad ingredients are far more nutritious than their cooked counterparts. This is because cooking can significantly reduce vitamin and antioxidant levels in many foods, including vegetables and nuts. You do not need to adopt a fully raw diet and forgo cooking entirely; incorporating just a few raw items into your meals can provide a great health boost.

Fruit and vegetables

When it comes to produce, fresh is best. Baby varieties of vegetables such as zucchini, carrots, and leeks are ideal, as they tend to be both sweeter and easier to digest. Keep in the fridge, preferably stored in a paper bag, as plastic bags make vegetables sweat.

Try these:

- Mediterranean salad boats (p143)
- ◀ **Waldorf salad (p158)**
- Orange salad with olives (p161)

Nuts and seeds

A handful of crunchy chopped walnuts or jewel-like pomegranate seeds can round out any salad dish. Some of the recipes in this book call for nuts to be roasted or dry-fried before serving, but you can skip that step and sprinkle them raw over the dish if you prefer.

Try these:

- ◀ **Nutty goat cheese and beet salad (p89)**
- Jeweled couscous and apricot salad (p92)
- Shredded carrot and cabbage with nuts (p148)

Using precooked foods

Round out a salad in no time with a selection of precooked foods from your fridge and pantry. Smoked fish, cured meats, and rich cheeses provide a particularly special depth of flavor to any meal, while a can of pulses or grains instantly adds bulk and fiber.

Smoked fish

Smoking imparts a delicious woody flavor to fish such as salmon, trout, and mackerel. It can be bought fresh or vacuum-packed, and you only need to flake a little over each salad to make an impact. Vacuum-packed smoked fish should be consumed within 2 days of opening, If bought loose, eat within 4 days.

Try these:

◀ **Smoked trout and endive with dill relish (p26)**

- Smoked salmon salad with spiced yogurt (p27)
- Smoked fish, fennel, and mango salad (p31)

Cooked and cured meats

Buy cooked meats from a delicatessen wherever possible, as these will be fresher and tastier than their prepackaged counterparts. Salted, dried, and smoked meats are also available from delicatessens. Keep all cooked and cured meat stored in the fridge, well away from raw meat, and use within 3–5 days.

Try these:

- Prosciutto with pear and nectarine (p59)
- Nutty bresaola salad with horseradish dressing (p62)

◀ **Pastrami and arugula salad with olive salsa (p63)**

Cheese

Use traditionally made cheeses for salads rather than cheaper packaged cheese—the flavor is far richer, meaning you don't need to use as much. If you have time, allow refrigerated cheese to come up to room temperature before serving.

Try these:

◀ **Tomato salad with balsamic vinegar (p82)**

- Gorgonzola and ciabatta salad (p83)
- Goat cheese and beans with chive dressing (p87)

Canned grains and pulses

Canned grains and pulses are precooked and stored in liquid, meaning they are ready to eat right away. Choose varieties that have been stored in water. Once opened, canned grains and pulses should be transferred to a nonmetallic container, refrigerated, and used within 2 days.

Try these:

◀ **Lentil, artichoke, and red pepper salad (p118)**

- Gingered fava beans with lentils (p120)
- Curried chickpeas with mango (p122)

On-the-go salads

Adapting a salad recipe into a portable meal, ready to take with you to work or school, couldn't be easier. Follow these steps to create a lunchbox-ready salad that remains as fresh and crisp as the moment you assembled it.

Choose your container

Both standard lunchboxes and modern salad jars can be used to contain your on-the-go salad. Whatever you use, ensure it has a watertight, noncorrosive seal and is thoroughly sterilized before use.

Layering components

Building an on-the-go salad requires separating ingredients into individual layers, then adding them into your on-the-go container in a certain order (see opposite). Keep liquids and heavy components at the bottom, topped by lighter items that you wish to remain crisp.

Keep it cool

Always keep on-the-go salads chilled, or preferably refrigerated—especially if it contains meat or fish. If your office or school does not provide access to a fridge, do not add meat or fish to your salad.

Layering an on-the-go salad

To keep an on-the-go salad fresh and crisp, it is a good idea to layer the components individually in the container, mixing them up only when you are ready to eat. Follow the steps below to adapt your favorite salad recipes into portable meals.

On-the-go icons

Look out for the "on the go" diagrams that accompany many of the recipes in this book. Each one is a simple, at-a-glance guide to adapting a salad recipe into a portable meal, complete with hints and tips for keeping your salad components as fresh as possible.

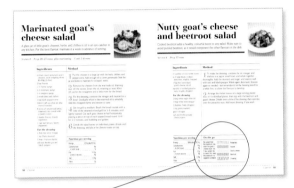

Follow the order below from 1 to 5 when assembling your on-the-go salad. If you are unsure where a certain component should go, remember that, as a general rule, any moist or heavy items should usually be added to the container first.

5

Salad leaves
These go in last, to ensure the delicate greens are not crushed by any other ingredients.

4

Toppings
Add a sprinkle of crunch and texture with a scattering of nuts, seeds, or dry fruits.

3

Lighter components
Use your judgment when adding softer items, such as cheese, fresh fruit, and cooked vegetables.

2

Heavier components
Grains, pasta, and dense vegetables are added next. These will soak into the dressing, so don't add anything here you intend to remain crunchy.

1

Dressing
Pour liquid into the container first, so that crisp ingredients can remain high and dry above it.

Combined salads

While most salads should be layered, some recipes are all-in-one meals, meaning that the ingredients are cooked together, and cannot be separated. These salads should be completely cool before being added to an on-the-go lunch container.

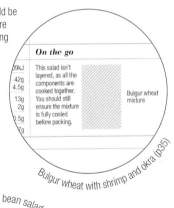

Bulgur wheat with shrimp and okra (p35)

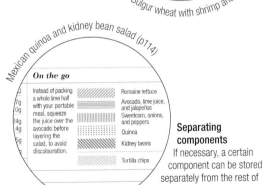

Mexican quinoa and kidney bean salad (p114)

Separating components

If necessary, a certain component can be stored separately from the rest of the salad to ensure everything remains crisp and dry. This may mean pouring a dressing into its own watertight bowl, or keeping bread or tortilla chips in another container.

Salad skills

While most salads require little more than assembling a selection of ingredients, mastering a few simple techniques can greatly improve the taste and presentation of your finished dishes. All the skills shown here are featured in several recipes in this book.

Segment citrus fruits

1 With a sharp knife, cut off the top and bottom of the fruit. Slice down and around the flesh, following the contour of the skin. Try to remove as much of the white pith as possible.

2 Slice along the lines of each membrane, which separate the slices, until you have removed the segments.

Prepare a mango

1 Slice through the mango, running your knife just to one side of the seed. Repeat on the other side, so that a single slice remains with the seed enclosed.

2 Cut into the flesh of the halves both lengthwise and crosswise. Do not cut through the skin. Then invert to expose the flesh, and slice off the cubes.

Peel and dice an onion

1 Cut in half lengthwise, leaving the root to hold the layers together. Peel.

2 Horizontally slice a half laid cut-side down. Do not slice through the root.

3 Slice down vertically, then hold the root and cut across the slices to dice.

Peel and chop garlic

1 Place each clove under a wide knife blade. Press down with your hand.

2 Discard the cracked skin and cut off the ends of each clove.

3 Slice into slivers lengthwise, then cut across into tiny chunks.

Chop herbs

1 Remove all stems and gather the leaves together in a tight pile or roll.

2 Slice the pile with a sharp knife, holding the leaves carefully in place.

3 Regather a pile and chop through the strips using a rocking motion.

Pit and peel avocados

1 Use a sharp knife to slice into the avocado and around the pit. Twist the halves in opposite directions and separate.

2 Strike the cutting edge of the knife into the pit. Lift the knife, wiggling if necessary, to remove it from the fruit.

3 Use a wooden spoon to carefully release the pit from the knife. Discard the pit.

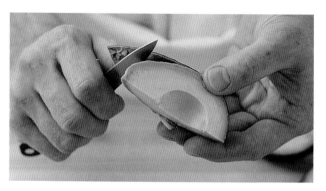

4 Quarter the avocado and use a paring knife to peel away and discard the skin. Slice or dice as needed.

Trim greens

1 Discard all limp, discolored leaves. Slice each leaf along both sides of the center rib, then remove it and discard.

2 Roll a few leaves together loosely into a bunch. Cut across the roll to the desired width, making strips.

Peel tomatoes

1 Remove the stem, score an "X" on the base, then boil for 20 seconds.

2 With a small sieve, transfer from the boiling water into ice water.

3 When cool enough to handle, use a knife to peel the loosened skin.

Char and peel peppers

1 Using tongs, hold over an open flame to char the skin all over.

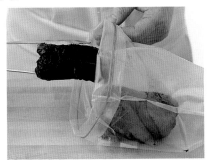

2 Put into a plastic bag, seal, and set aside to allow the skins to loosen.

3 Once they have completely cooled, peel away the charred skin.

Seed and dice chiles

1 Cut in half lengthwise. Scrape out the seeds and remove the pith.

2 Flatten each chile half with your hand and slice as needed.

3 For a fine dice, turn the slices horizontally and cut across.

Fish and seafood

With nutritionists recommending we eat two portions of fish a week, including one of oily fish, these salad recipes offer an easy and healthy route to increasing your omega-3 intake.

Herbed mackerel salad

Throw together this fragrant salad for a light meal packed with flavor—and then mop up the dressing with a crispy baguette. Smoked mackerel is great to have in the fridge because it's quick, inexpensive, and high in protein.

Serves 4   Prep 10–15 mins   Cook 15–20 mins

Ingredients

salt and freshly ground
  black pepper

1¼lb (550g) new potatoes,
  well scrubbed and chopped
  into bite-sized chunks

7oz (200g) hot-smoked
  mackerel fillets, skinned

2oz (60g) baby salad leaves

2 tbsp chopped dill

2 tbsp chopped chives

7oz (200g) cooked beets
  (not in vinegar), roughly
  chopped

baguette, to serve

For the dressing

¼ cup extra-virgin olive oil

juice of 1 lemon

1 tsp whole-grain mustard

1 tsp honey

1 garlic clove, finely chopped

Method

1 Bring a large pot of salted water to a boil. Add the potato chunks and cook for 10–15 minutes, or until tender. Drain and set aside.

2 Meanwhile, break the mackerel into bite-sized pieces, removing any bones you find as you go, and place in a large serving bowl. Add the salad leaves and herbs, and gently toss together.

3 Place the dressing ingredients in a small bowl, season, and whisk together with a fork.

4 Add the warm potatoes to the serving bowl, pour in the dressing, and stir gently. Add the beets and serve immediately with the baguette.

Nutrition per serving

Energy	279cals (1167kJ)
Carbohydrate	26g
of which sugar	6g
Fat	12g
of which saturated	2.5g
Sodium	1.1g
Fiber	4g

On the go

Let the potatoes cool before you add them to the container with the dressing, then layer in the remaining ingredients.

//////////	Salad leaves
==========	Mackerel
\\\\\\\\\\	Beets
::::::::::	Potatoes
||||||||||	Dressing and herbs

Tuna, artichoke, and pasta salad

A hearty meal-in-one salad, this dish is enhanced by a few pantry ingredients and some fresh green beans. It's packed with flavor and pretty enough to share. Prepare ahead for a tasty weekday packed lunch.

Serves 4   Prep 15 mins   Cook 10 mins

Ingredients

salt and freshly ground
  black pepper

7¾oz (220g) pasta, such
  as penne or fusilli

3½oz (100g) thin green beans,
  trimmed and halved

1 × 7oz (200g) can tuna in
  spring water, drained and flaked

1 × 14oz (400g) can cannellini
  beans, drained and rinsed

10 sun-dried tomatoes in oil,
  drained and roughly chopped
  (oil reserved)

1 × 9oz (250g) jar artichoke hearts
  in oil, drained (oil reserved)

finely grated zest and juice
  of 1 lemon

1 tsp whole-grain mustard

3 tbsp chopped flat-leaf
  parsley

leaves from 3 sprigs of basil, torn

Method

1 Bring a large pot of salted water to a boil. Cook the pasta according to the package instructions, adding the green beans 4–5 minutes before the end of the cooking time. Drain and rinse under cold running water until the pasta is cold. Drain well and place in a serving dish. Add the tuna, cannellini beans, sun-dried tomatoes, and artichokes and toss to combine.

2 Place 3 tablespoons of the oil from the sun-dried tomatoes and 3 tablespoons of the oil from the drained artichokes in a small bowl. Stir in the lemon zest, lemon juice, and mustard, along with any seasoning.

3 Pour the dressing over the pasta. Add the herbs and toss well to coat. Cover and chill until ready to serve.

Nutrition per serving	
Energy	458cals (1802kJ)
Carbohydrate	51g
of which sugar	3.5g
Fat	15g
of which saturated	2g
Sodium	1.7g
Fiber	13g

On the go

Keep the tuna near the top of the container so the delicate fish doesn't disintegrate in transit.

- Herbs
- Tuna
- Pasta
- Vegetables
- Cannellini beans
- Dressing

Mediterranean tuna and farro salad

Farro is an ancient grain, similar in texture to pearl barley. Enjoyed in Italy for its distinctive nutty taste, it pairs perfectly with tuna and tomatoes to create a hearty salad that will transport your senses to southern Europe.

Serves 4   Prep 15 mins   Cook 30 mins

Ingredients

½ cup uncooked farro

2 x 5oz (160g) cans tuna in spring water or brine, drained

5 sun-dried tomatoes in oil, roughly chopped

2½oz (70g) green olives, pitted and halved

1 small red onion, diced

1 small red bell pepper, seeded and cut into bite-sized pieces

1 small zucchini, cut into bite-sized pieces

3½oz (100g) mixed salad leaves

¼ cup chopped basil, to garnish

For the dressing

3 tbsp extra-virgin olive oil

2 tbsp balsamic vinegar

½ tsp Italian seasoning

1 garlic clove, crushed

salt and freshly ground black pepper (optional)

Method

1 Place the farro in a large saucepan and cover with water. Bring to a boil, and then reduce the heat to a simmer. Cook for about 30 minutes or until tender. Remove from the heat, drain any remaining water, and leave to cool.

2 Use a fork to roughly flake the tuna from the cans and place in a large bowl. Add the tomatoes, olives, onions, red pepper, and zucchini and mix well. Then add the cooled farro and mix until well combined.

3 For the dressing, place the oil, vinegar, seasoning, and garlic in a bowl and whisk to combine. Taste and season with salt and pepper, if needed. Place the salad leaves on plates. Top with the tuna and farro mixture and pour in the dressing. Toss lightly to coat and garnish with basil. Serve immediately.

Nutrition per serving	
Energy	359cals (1475kJ)
Carbohydrate	23g
of which sugar	7g
Fat	19g
of which saturated	2.5g
Sodium	1.4g
Fiber	3.5g

On the go

Drain both the tuna and sun-dried tomatoes well, so excess liquid doesn't soften the salad or dilute the dressing.

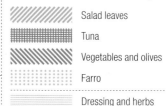

Salad leaves

Tuna

Vegetables and olives

Farro

Dressing and herbs

Smoked trout salad
with pickled cucumber

Homemade pickled cucumber is surprisingly quick and easy to make. Its refreshing tang adds a lift to any dish it is paired with—including this light salad of smoked fish and avocado.

Serves 4   Prep 15 mins

Ingredients

1 avocado, halved, pitted, and peeled

juice of 1 lemon

4 tbsp Greek-style yogurt

handful of mint leaves, chopped

2 large handfuls of mixed salad leaves

12 green olives, pitted

2 × 7oz (200g) cold-smoked trout fillets, flaked

salt and freshly ground black pepper

For the pickled cucumber

2 tbsp white wine vinegar

2 tsp sugar

1 fresh red chile, seeded and finely chopped

½ large cucumber, peeled and halved lengthwise, seeded, and sliced

Method

1 Cut the avocado flesh into slices lengthwise, then sprinkle with the lemon juice to prevent discoloration. Set aside.

2 To make the pickled cucumber, whisk the vinegar, sugar, and chile in a small bowl until combined. Add the cucumber, and toss it all together. In a separate small bowl, stir together the yogurt and mint until well mixed.

3 Arrange the salad leaves and olives in a large bowl or on 4 individual plates. Top with the flaked trout and avocado, then season to taste. Spoon some of the pickled cucumber mixture over top, and keep the rest in a bowl to serve on the side along with the mint yogurt.

Nutrition per serving

Energy	259cals (1055kJ)
Carbohydrate	5g
of which sugar	4g
Fat	15.5g
of which saturated	4g
Sodium	2.5g
Fiber	3g

Niçoise-style salad

A culinary classic, the traditional "salade niçoise" is instantly recognizable thanks to its combination of olives, tuna, and tomatoes. Our version doesn't include hard-boiled eggs, but you can throw a few in for extra protein if you wish.

Serves 4   Prep 15 mins

Ingredients

1 cup fava beans, fresh (out of their pods) or frozen

salt and freshly ground black pepper

2 × 6oz (175g) cans tuna in olive oil, drained

10 cherry tomatoes, halved

handful of fresh flat-leaf parsley, finely chopped

bunch of fresh chives, finely chopped

12 black olives, pitted

12 salt-packed anchovies, rinsed, or flat anchovies in oil, drained

1 head of crisp lettuce, such as romaine, leaves separated

2–3 scallions, thinly sliced

For the dressing

6 tbsp extra-virgin olive oil

2 tbsp white wine vinegar

2 garlic cloves, grated or finely chopped

1–2 tsp Dijon mustard

Method

1 If using frozen fava beans, soak them in hot water for 5 minutes, then drain.

2 To make the dressing, put all the dressing ingredients in a screw-top jar, season well with salt and black pepper, cover with the lid, and shake to blend.

3 Put the tuna and tomatoes in a bowl, and drizzle with half of the dressing. Sprinkle in half of the fresh herbs, and season generously with salt and black pepper. Toss together. Now add the drained fava beans, olives, and anchovies, and mix gently.

4 Line a bowl with the lettuce leaves, and arrange the tuna mixture on top. Drizzle with the remaining dressing, and sprinkle over the remaining herbs. Top with the scallions, and serve.

Nutrition per serving	
Energy	376cals (1537kJ)
Carbohydrate	4g
of which sugar	2g
Fat	26g
of which saturated	3.5g
Sodium	2.6g
Fiber	4g

On the go

Roughly chop or shred the lettuce leaves before adding it to the top of your salad. Don't overfill the container.

Lettuce

Tuna and tomatoes

Olives and anchovies

Fava beans

Dressing and herbs

Smoked trout and endive *with dill relish*

Also known as chicory, endive has a mild bitter taste and a crisp, crunchy texture. Drizzling lemon juice over the leaves not only adds extra flavor, but also prevents discoloration while you prepare the rest of the dish.

Serves 4   Prep 15 mins

Ingredients

3–4 tsp horseradish cream

½ red onion, finely diced

1–2 heads curly endive, leaves separated and rinsed

2 large cold-smoked trout fillets, about 8oz (225g) each, flaked

drizzle of olive oil

juice of ½ lemon

salt and freshly ground black pepper

For the dressing

2–3 apples

2 cooked bees (not in vinegar), chopped

handful of fresh dill, finely chopped

Method

1 In a small bowl, mix together the horseradish and half of the onion. Set aside.

2 Arrange the endive and flaked trout on a serving plate, and drizzle with the oil and lemon juice. Season with salt and some black pepper.

3 To make the relish, peel, core, and chop the apples into bite-sized pieces. Place in a separate bowl with the beets and dill, and mix together.

4 To serve, spoon the relish over the leaves and fish. Sprinkle over the remaining red onion, and serve with the horseradish-onion mixture on the side.

Nutrition per serving

Energy	246cals (996kJ)
Carbohydrate	14g
of which sugar	13g
Fat	9g
of which saturated	2g
Sodium	2.7g
Fiber	3g

Smoked salmon salad *with spiced yogurt*

Salads are often accused of being bland and boring. However, no one will say that when you serve up this colorful creation, featuring red chile, capers, and a dash of five-spice powder.

Serves 4   Prep 15 mins

Ingredients

3 tomatoes

1 tbsp capers, rinsed, gently squeezed dry, and chopped

handful of radishes, diced

1 orange bell pepper, seeded and diced

4 scallions, finely chopped

1 fresh red chile, seeded and finely chopped

juice of 1 large orange

juice of 1 lime

salt and freshly ground black pepper

9oz (250g) smoked salmon, chopped into bite-sized pieces

For the dressing

4–6 tbsp Greek-style yogurt

juice of 1 lemon

pinch of five-spice powder

Method

1 First, peel the tomatoes (see p15). Cut each tomato in half and squeeze over a bowl to remove the seeds, then slice into cubes.

2 In a large bowl, mix together the tomatoes, capers, radishes, bell pepper, scallions, and chile. Add the orange and lime juices, and season with salt and black pepper. Toss gently to mix, and let stand for about 10 minutes to develop the flavors.

3 To make the spiced yogurt dressing, mix together the yogurt, lemon juice, and five-spice powder in a small bowl. Season to taste.

4 When ready to serve, add the smoked salmon pieces to the salad mixture, and toss again. Serve with the spiced yogurt on the side.

Nutrition per serving

Energy	172cals (710kJ)
Carbohydrate	7g
of which sugar	7g
Fat	8.5g
of which saturated	3g
Sodium	1.6g
Fiber	2g

Salmon salad
with raspberry dressing

Using a tangy, fruity dressing adds a bit of unexpected pizzazz to this dish and cuts through the rich salmon. Try it in a variety of salads as a substitute for more common vinaigrettes.

Serves 4   Prep 10 mins   Cook 25 mins

Ingredients

salt and freshly ground
  black pepper

4 salmon fillets, about 14oz
  (400g) total

1 tbsp olive oil

few stalks of fresh thyme,
  leaves only

½ cup fava beans, fresh (out of
  their pods) or frozen

9oz (250g) baby spinach leaves

¼ cup roasted hazelnuts,
  roughly chopped

½ cup reduced-fat feta cheese,
  crumbled

For dressing

3 tbsp olive oil

1 tbsp raspberry vinegar

Method

1 Preheat the oven to 350°F (180°C). Whisk the dressing ingredients together, season well with salt and pepper, then set aside to develop the flavors.

2 Arrange the salmon fillets in a roasting pan, drizzle with the olive oil, and scatter the thyme leaves over top. Season with salt and pepper and bake in the oven for 15 minutes until the fish is cooked and flakes easily. Remove from the oven and set aside to cool.

3 Cook the fava beans in a pot of boiling salted water for 8 minutes or until tender, then drain, refresh with cold water, and drain again. Arrange the spinach leaves on a plate, and top with the flaked fish and fava beans. Sprinkle over the hazelnuts and feta and drizzle with the dressing when ready to serve.

Nutrition per serving

Energy	752cals (3118kJ)
Carbohydrate	6g
of which sugar	3g
Fat	56g
of which saturated	10g
Sodium	10g
Fiber	6g

On the go

By adding the spinach last, you keep the leaves separate from the dressing so that they don't wilt before lunchtime.

- Spinach
- Feta cheese
- Salmon
- Fava beans and hazelnuts
- Dressing

Spring rice salad with smoked salmon

In this salad, the freshness of the asparagus works well with the rich flavor and buttery texture of the salmon. The flavors develop when left to chill in the refrigerator, making it perfect for an office lunch.

Serves 4–6   Prep 20–25 mins, plus chilling   Cook 15–20 mins

Ingredients

salt and freshly ground black pepper

1 lemon, cut in half

1 cup long-grain rice

2 cups asparagus spears

3 celery stalks, peeled and diced

9oz (250g) smoked salmon, cut into strips

For the dressing

3 tbsp tarragon vinegar

2 tsp Dijon mustard

¾ cup vegetable oil

Method

1 First, make the dressing. Whisk together the vinegar and mustard in a small bowl, and season. Gradually whisk in the oil in a thin stream to thicken and emulsify the dressing.

2 Bring a large pot of salted water to a boil. Squeeze the juice from one lemon half into the water, then drop in the squeezed lemon half. Add the rice, stir, and bring back to a boil. Simmer for 10–12 minutes, stirring occasionally, until the rice is tender. Drain the rice through a sieve, and discard the lemon half. Rinse the rice with cold water and thoroughly drain again, to wash away the starch. Transfer to a large bowl.

3 Bring another pot of salted water to a boil. Add the asparagus and simmer for 5–7 minutes, until tender. Drain and cut the stalks into chunky pieces.

4 Whisk the vinaigrette again and pour it over the rice. Stir well and add the asparagus, celery, salmon, and remaining lemon juice. Toss together and season. Cover and chill for at least 1 hour. Serve at room temperature.

Nutrition per serving

Energy 615–410cals (2550–1700kJ)	
Carbohydrate	40–26.5g
of which sugar	1.5–1g
Fat	40–26.5g
of which saturated	5.5–3.7g
Sodium	2.2–1.5g
Fiber	1.7–1.2g

On the go

The rice will mix with the dressing in the bottom of the container, infusing the salad with tarragon.

Smoked salmon

Celery and asparagus

Rice

Dressing

Smoked fish, fennel, and mango salad

Fruit and fish might not immediately seem like the most obvious culinary combination, but it really does work. In this recipe, mango and pomegranate pair perfectly with the mix of mackerel and trout, creating a light, refreshing meal.

Serves 4   Prep 15 mins

Ingredients

salt and freshly ground
  black pepper

10oz (300g) smoked mackerel

5½oz (150g) smoked trout

1 fennel bulb, trimmed
  and peeled into thin strips

1 mango, pitted, peeled, and
  sliced

seeds of 1 pomegranate

For the dressing

⅓ cup extra-virgin
  olive oil

3 tbsp red wine vinegar

2 garlic cloves, grated or
  finely chopped

pinch of sugar

handful of fresh dill,
  finely chopped

Method

1 First, make the dressing. Put all the ingredients in a small bowl, and whisk together until well blended. Season with salt and black pepper.

2 Flake the mackerel into bite-sized chunks, and slice the trout into chunky strips. Arrange the fish on a plate, add the fennel and mango slices, and sprinkle over the pomegranate seeds.

3 When ready to serve, drizzle with the dressing, and serve with slices of fresh whole-wheat or other dark bread.

Nutrition per serving

Energy	480cals (1952kJ)
Carbohydrate	11g
of which sugar	10.5g
Fat	37g
of which saturated	7g
Sodium	2.3g
Fiber	4g

Chile shrimp with cilantro and lime

This dish may look delicate, but the cilantro and chiles pack a real punch. Serve it as it is for a quick starter or side, or toss with some extra salad leaves or diced bell peppers for something a little more substantial.

Serves 4   Prep 15 mins

Ingredients

16 cooked shrimp, peeled and deveined, tails left on

handful of fresh cilantro, finely chopped

1–2 fresh red chiles, seeded and finely chopped

1 × 14oz (400g) can lima beans, drained and rinsed

2 handfuls of arugula

juice of 1 lime

salt and freshly ground black pepper

splash of hot-sweet chili sauce, such as sriracha

Method

1 Put the shrimp in a large bowl. Mix in half of the cilantro and the fresh chiles. Add in the lima beans, and toss to mix again.

2 Arrange the arugula in a large serving bowl or on 4 individual plates. Sprinkle over some of the lime juice, and season with pinch of salt and some black pepper. Stir the remaining lime juice into the shrimp mixture, then taste and adjust the seasoning as needed.

3 Spoon the shrimp mixture over the arugula, drizzle with the hot-sweet chili sauce, and sprinkle over the remaining cilantro. Serve immediately.

If you would like to soften the lima beans a little before using, put them in a bowl and cover with hot water. Let stand for 10 minutes, then drain well.

Nutrition per serving

Energy	128cals (506kJ)
Carbohydrate	12g
of which sugar	4.5g
Fat	0.7g
of which saturated	0.2g
Sodium	1.4g
Fiber	4g

Bulgur wheat with shrimp and okra

This sensational dish can be eaten hot or cold. It would make a great addition to any buffet or dinner party—and any leftovers would make an excellent all-in-one portable lunch.

Serves 8   Prep 15 mins   Cook 30 mins

Ingredients

2½ cups bulgur wheat

½ cup extra-virgin olive oil

2 large onions, finely chopped

1lb (450g) okra, trimmed and cut into chunks

6 garlic cloves, peeled and grated, or finely chopped

1½lb (675g) shelled and deveined large shrimp

½ cup dry white wine

large handful of dill, chopped

salt and freshly ground black pepper

Method

1 Preheat the oven to 300°F (150°C). Put the bulgur wheat in a heatproof bowl, and pour in enough boiling water to cover. Cover the bowl with a kitchen towel, leave for 5 minutes, then stir.

2 Meanwhile, heat the oil in a large saucepan, add the onions, and cook over medium heat for 5 minutes, or until they start to soften. Add the okra and cook for 2 minutes, then add the garlic and shrimp and continue to cook, stirring frequently, for 2–3 minutes or until the shrimp have just started to turn pink.

3 Stir in the wine and dill, and cook for 2 minutes, then stir in the bulgur. Transfer to an ovenproof serving dish, season with salt and pepper, and cover with foil. Bake, stirring occasionally, for 20 minutes, or until heated through. Serve hot or cold.

Nutrition per serving

Energy	400cals (1609kJ)
Carbohydrate	42g
of which sugar	4.5g
Fat	13g
of which saturated	2g
Sodium	0.5g
Fiber	7g

On the go

This salad isn't layered, as all the components are cooked together. You should still ensure the mixture is fully cooled before packing.

Bulgur wheat mixture

Vietnamese shrimp and cucumber salad

The classic Vietnamese flavors of lime, chiles, and mint combine here to produce a wonderful summer salad. Be sure to obtain fish sauce, as it is vital to the taste of the finished dish.

Serves 4   Prep 15 mins   Cook 2–3 mins

Ingredients

12 large raw shrimp, peeled and deveined, with heads and tails removed

2 tbsp vegetable oil

1 tsp rice wine vinegar

1 tsp sugar

1 red chile, seeded and very finely chopped

2 garlic cloves, crushed

2 tbsp Vietnamese fish sauce (nuac nam) or Thai fish sauce (nam pla)

1 tbsp lime juice

1 tbsp chopped Vietnamese mint (rau ram) or other fresh mint leaves, plus a few sprigs to serve

1 green papaya, peeled, seeded, quartered lengthwise, and thinly sliced

½ cucumber, seeded and cut into thin strips

Method

1 Spread the shrimp out on a foil-lined grill rack, brush with the oil, and grill over medium heat for 2–3 minutes, or until they turn pink.

2 Meanwhile, whisk the rice wine vinegar, sugar, chile, garlic, fish sauce, lime juice, and 2½fl oz (75ml) cold water together in a bowl until the sugar dissolves. Add the cooked shrimp to the bowl and stir until they are coated in the dressing. Let cool completely.

3 Add the chopped rau ram or mint, papaya, and cucumber, and toss together. Transfer the salad to a serving plate, with the shrimp on the top, and garnish with mint sprigs.

Nutrition per serving

Energy	149cals (634kJ)
Carbohydrate	5.5g
of which sugar	2g
Fat	6.5g
of which saturated	0.8g
Sodium	2.5g
Fiber	2g

Grilled squid and arugula salad

It is best to barbecue this chile squid to guarantee maximum flavor, but using a grill pan works well, too. If you don't want to clean the squid yourself, ask your fishmonger to prepare it for you—although this may cost extra.

Serves 4   Prep 15 mins   Cook 2 mins

Ingredients

1lb 5oz (600g) whole squid (choose small young squid, rather than one large one)

4 tbsp olive oil

2 small fresh red chiles, seeded and finely chopped

1 garlic clove, crushed

2 lemons

salt and freshly ground black pepper

3½oz (100g) arugula

large handful of fresh flat-leaf parsley, roughly chopped

2 tbsp olive oil

Method

1 Clean the squid by grabbing the head and tentacles together in one hand, and pulling them out of the body. Cut the head from the tentacles and discard, making sure that the tentacles remain attached as one. Cut or pull out the small beak from inside the tentacles. Pull out and discard the strip of transparent cartilage from inside the body, and rinse the body (the thin outer skin should peel away) and tentacles thoroughly. Pat dry with paper towels.

2 Put the tentacles and bodies (tubes and wings attached) in a large bowl with the olive oil, chiles, and garlic, along with the grated zest and juice of 1 lemon. Season with salt and black pepper.

3 Heat the grill of a barbecue or charcoal grill until hot. Grill the squid bodies and tentacles over high heat for 1–2 minutes, turning halfway through cooking, until lightly charred on all sides. Transfer to a cutting board. Cut the tentacle clusters in half crosswise and put in a serving bowl. Slice the tubes into ⅛in (3mm) rings, slicing through the wings as you go, and place in the bowl with the tentacles.

4 Slice the remaining lemon in half. Put the arugula, parsley, olive oil, and juice of 1 lemon half in the bowl and toss gently with the squid. Serve with lemon wedges cut from the remaining lemon half.

Nutrition per serving

Energy	269cals (1146kJ)
Carbohydrate	0g
of which sugar	0g
Fat	19g
of which saturated	3g
Sodium	0.4g
Fiber	0.5g

Mixed seafood salad
with anchovy dressing

Most supermarkets offer packs of precooked seafood, which are handy when you need a quick family dinner. Simply throw this salad together in a large serving bowl, toss with the dressing, and let everybody help themselves.

Serves 4   Prep 15 mins

Ingredients

handful of mixed salad leaves, such as romaine

1 fennel bulb, thinly sliced

1lb (450g) assorted cooked seafood, such as shelled shrimp, mussels, or squid rings, rinsed and dried

6 whole anchovies in oil, drained

1 fresh hot green chile, seeded and finely chopped

handful of fresh cilantro, roughly chopped

lemon wedges, to serve

rice noodles, to serve

For the dressing

3 tbsp extra-virgin olive oil

1 tbsp white wine vinegar

6 whole anchovies in oil, drained and finely chopped

pinch of sugar

handful of fresh flat-leaf parsley, finely chopped

salt and freshly ground black pepper

Method

1 First, make the dressing. In a large bowl, whisk together the oil and vinegar. Add the anchovies, sugar, and parsley; season well with salt and black pepper; and whisk again.

2 In a bowl, toss together the salad leaves, fennel, seafood, anchovies, chile, and cilantro. Add the dressing, and toss again to coat. Place the salad into a shallow serving bowl, and serve with lemon wedges and rice noodles.

Rice noodles are easy to prepare—just soak them in hot water for about 10 minutes, then drain and serve.

Nutrition per serving	
Energy	193cals (844kJ)
Carbohydrate	2g
of which sugar	2g
Fat	11g
of which saturated	2g
Sodium	3.1g
Fiber	2.5g

On the go

Toss the noodles in the dressing before layering in the other ingredients to prevent them from sticking together.

Salad leaves and cilantro

Fennel and chile

Seafood and anchovies

Noodles

Dressing

Crab and grapefruit salad *with vinaigrette*

This is a wonderfully light and zesty salad. Fresh crabmeat is combined with the sweet-and-sour flavor of pink grapefruit, and finished with cilantro and a classic vinaigrette dressing.

Serves 4   Prep 10 mins

Ingredients

12oz (350g) fresh white
  crabmeat, cooked and
  drained

handful of baby salad leaves

handful of fresh cilantro

2 pink grapefruits, peeled,
  segmented, and pith removed

For the dressing

3 tbsp extra-virgin olive oil

1 tbsp white wine vinegar

pinch of sugar

sea salt and freshly ground
  black pepper

Method

1 In a small bowl, whisk together the dressing ingredients.
Season with salt and pepper.

2 In a separate bowl, mix the crabmeat with a drizzle of
the dressing. Divide the salad leaves and half of the
cilantro between 4 individual plates, and scatter over the
grapefruit segments.

3 When ready to serve, drizzle the salad with the
remaining dressing. Divide the crabmeat between
the plates, spooning it neatly on top of the leaves. Scatter
over the remaining cilantro and serve immediately.

Nutrition per serving

Energy	186cals (776kJ)
Carbohydrate	7g
of which sugar	7g
Fat	9g
of which saturated	1g
Sodium	0.7g
Fiber	2g

On the go

On its own, this salad makes a light lunch. Pack a slice of crusty seeded bread with your meal for a more filling on-the-go meal.

- Salad leaves
- Crabmeat
- Grapefruit
- Dressing

Chile crab and avocado salad

Fresh white crabmeat is a treat: here, it is pepped up with chiles and herbs and served with dressed salad leaves. Your fishmonger can shell the crab for you, but it will always be freshest if you prepare it yourself.

Serves 4   Prep 5 mins

Ingredients

10oz (300g) fresh white crabmeat

2 ripe avocados, peeled, pitted, and diced

½ cup chives, finely chopped

½ cup dill, finely chopped

½ cup parsley, finely chopped

½ red chile, seeded and finely chopped

salt and freshly ground black pepper

3½oz (100g) mixed salad leaves

4 lemon wedges, to serve

For the dressing

3 tbsp olive oil

1 tbsp apple cider vinegar

½ tsp paprika

2 tsp capers, finely chopped

½ tsp mayonnaise

Method

1 Put the crabmeat and avocados in a medium bowl along with the herbs and the chile, stir well, and season with salt and black pepper.

2 In a separate bowl, whisk together all the dressing ingredients. Taste the dressing and season, if necessary.

3 Lay the salad leaves on a serving plate or 4 individual plates and top with the crabmeat mixture. Drizzle with the dressing and serve with the lemon wedges.

You can prepare the crab mixture and dressing up to 1–2 hours ahead and keep them in the refrigerator, covered, until needed.

Nutrition per serving

Energy	323cals (1334kJ)
Carbohydrate	2g
of which sugar	0.5g
Fat	28g
of which saturated	5g
Sodium	1g
Fiber	2.5g

Poultry and meat

Salad doesn't have to mean vegetarian. Dig into
a selection of dishes featuring freshly grilled lamb
and beef, succulent chicken breast, and choice
samples of rich and flavorful deli meats.

Chicken, radicchio, and asparagus salad

This French "salade tiède," or warm salad, is easy to assemble and makes for a healthy dinner you can put together in minutes. You can buy jars of roasted bell peppers in most supermarkets, or prepare your own (see p15).

Serves 4   Prep 5–10 mins   Cook 10–15 mins

Ingredients

¼ cup olive oil

4 skinless chicken breasts, about 5½oz (150g) each, cut into thin strips

1 garlic clove, finely chopped

⅓ cup roasted red bell peppers, thinly sliced

salt and freshly ground black pepper

1 small head radicchio, torn into small pieces

2 cups asparagus spears, trimmed and cut into 3 pieces

2 tbsp raspberry vinegar

½ tsp sugar

Method

1 Heat 2 tablespoons of the oil in a large nonstick frying pan over medium-high heat. Add the chicken and garlic and cook, stirring, for 5–7 minutes, or until the chicken is tender and cooked through. Stir in the roasted red bell peppers, and season to taste with salt and pepper.

2 Meanwhile, put the radicchio in a large serving bowl. Remove the chicken from the pan using a slotted spoon and place in the bowl with the radicchio.

3 Add the asparagus to the fat remaining in the pan and fry, stirring constantly, for 1–2 minutes, or until just tender. Transfer to the bowl with the chicken.

4 Whisk together the remaining 2 tablespoons of the oil, the vinegar and sugar, then pour into the pan and stir over high heat until well combined. Pour this dressing over the salad and toss quickly so that all the ingredients are well mixed and coated with the dressing. Serve immediately.

Nutrition per serving

Energy	284cals (1190kJ)
Carbohydrate	3g
of which sugar	3g
Fat	13g
of which saturated	2g
Sodium	0.2g
Fiber	2g

On the go

All components of this salad should be fully cooled before layering. Keep the salad refrigerated before eating.

Radicchio

Roasted bell peppers

Asparagus

Chicken

Dressing

Chicken Caesar salad
with polenta croutons

Using fried polenta to make the crunchy croutons for this popular salad gives it a twist by providing extra texture to complement the succulence of the chicken and the freshness of the lettuce.

Serves 4   Prep 20 mins   Cook 10 mins

Ingredients

2 tbsp olive oil

1 cup polenta, cooked and cut into 1in (2.5cm) cubes

rock salt and freshly ground black pepper

1 large or 2 small heads romaine lettuce, washed, dried, and torn into bite-sized pieces

8oz (225g) cooked skinless chicken breasts or thighs, cut into bite-sized pieces

¾ cup freshly grated Romano cheese

For the dressing

½ cup extra-virgin olive oil

1 tbsp Dijon mustard

3 tbsp mayonnaise

4 anchovy fillets, chopped

½ tsp Worcestershire sauce

1 garlic clove, crushed

2 tbsp finely grated Parmesan cheese, plus extra to serve

pinch of sugar

Method

1 Heat the oil in a large frying pan over medium heat. Add the polenta and season. Cook for 10 minutes, turning over the polenta cubes occasionally, until lightly browned and crisp. Remove from the heat and set aside.

2 For the dressing, place all the ingredients in a food processor and pulse until emulsified into a thick and creamy dressing. Season with pepper, mix well to combine, and set aside.

3 Place the lettuce, chicken, and cheese in a large bowl and toss lightly to combine. Drizzle with the dressing a little at a time, and toss until well coated. Arrange the salad on a serving dish and scatter the polenta croutons over it. Sprinkle over some Parmesan and serve immediately.

Nutrition per serving

Energy	521cals (2180kJ)
Carbohydrate	1.5g
of which sugar	1.5g
Fat	44g
of which saturated	10g
Sodium	1.5g
Fiber	0.8g

On the go

Refrigerate the polenta croutons before layering this salad, so they remain firm while packed in the container.

- Cheese
- Lettuce
- Polenta
- Chicken
- Dressing

Chicken with adzuki beans and parsley

Adzuki beans originally come from East Asia, where they are often sweetened and used in desserts. This simple recipe offers a sugar-free way to enjoy these pulses, pairing them with chicken and a simple vinaigrette dressing.

Serves 4   Prep 10 mins

Ingredients

½ large red onion, finely diced

1 × 14oz (400g) can adzuki beans, drained and rinsed

1 tsp whole-grain mustard

white wine vinegar

extra-virgin olive oil

salt and freshly ground black pepper

handful of fresh flat-leaf parsley, finely chopped

12oz (350g) cooked skinless chicken breasts or thighs, shredded

Method

1 Mix together the onion (reserving a little to garnish the salad), beans, and mustard in a bowl. Add a splash of vinegar and a drizzle of olive oil, and season with salt and black pepper. Stir in the parsley.

2 Spoon the bean mixture into a shallow serving bowl, then top with the shredded chicken. Sprinkle over the remaining red onion, and serve with some fresh crusty bread and arugula.

Nutrition per serving

Energy	225cals (900kJ)
Carbohydrate	11g
of which sugar	1.5g
Fat	5g
of which saturated	1g
Sodium	0.2g
Fiber	6g

On the go

This salad can benefit from a touch of green when enjoyed as an on-the-go lunch; a handful of peppery arugula will do.

/////////	Arugula
=========	Red onion
||||||||||||	Shredded chicken
:::::::::::	Adzuki bean mixture

Chicken and peanut kamut salad

Peanut butter in a salad—who would have thought it was possible? Together with kamut, an ancient Egyptian grain, the peanuts lend a nutty taste to this salad, which is balanced perfectly with zesty lime juice.

Serves 2   *Prep 10 mins, plus soaking*   *Cook 45 mins*

Ingredients

¾ cup uncooked kamut

10oz (300g) cooked skinless chicken breasts or thighs, shredded

4 scallions, finely chopped

salt and freshly ground black pepper

2 tbsp salted peanuts

2 tbsp chopped cilantro, to garnish

For the dressing

2 tbsp smooth peanut butter

juice of 1 lime

Method

1 Place the kamut in a large bowl and cover with water. Let soak for 8 hours or for up to 24 hours. Then drain, rinse under running water, and drain well again.

2 Place the kamut in a large pot, cover with water, and bring to a boil. Then reduce the heat to a simmer and cook for 40–45 minutes. Remove from the heat and drain any remaining water. Set aside and keep warm.

3 For the dressing, place the peanut butter and lime juice in a small bowl. Add 2 tablespoons of water and whisk until well combined and thickened to the consistency of heavy cream.

4 Place the warm kamut in a large bowl. Add the chicken and scallions and toss lightly to mix. Then drizzle with the dressing, season to taste, and toss well to coat. Sprinkle over the peanuts, garnish with cilantro, and serve immediately.

Nutrition per serving

Energy	672cals (2776kJ)
Carbohydrate	64g
of which sugar	3g
Fat	20g
of which saturated	4.5g
Sodium	0.5g
Fiber	2g

On the go

Don't go out and buy precooked chicken; use your Sunday leftovers to build this salad for your Monday lunch.

Peanuts and cilantro

Scallions

Chicken

Kamut

Dressing

Spicy chicken salad with raw vegetables

This colorful salad requires very little cooking. If you prefer, you can spiralize the vegetables instead of shaving them—this will give them a more noodlelike appearance. Toss with the dressing at the last minute to prevent wilting.

Serves 4   Prep 10 mins   Cook 7–10 mins

Ingredients

14oz (400g) boneless, skinless chicken breasts

salt

juice of 2 limes

4 tsp Thai fish sauce

1 tbsp sugar

pinch of red pepper flakes (optional)

1 small head lettuce, shredded

¼lb (100g) ready-to-eat bean sprouts

1 large carrot, shaved using a vegetable peeler

1 × 6in (15cm) piece of cucumber, seeded and thinly sliced

½ red bell pepper, thinly sliced

½ yellow bell pepper, thinly sliced

15 cherry tomatoes, halved

handful of mint leaves, chopped

handful of cilantro, chopped

5 tbsp salted peanuts, chopped (optional)

Method

1 Poach the chicken in a large pot in plenty of simmering salted water for 7–10 minutes, depending on the thickness, until cooked through. Let cool, then thinly slice.

2 In a bowl, whisk the lime juice, fish sauce, sugar, a pinch of salt, and the red pepper flakes, if using, until the sugar dissolves.

3 In a serving bowl, mix together the salad vegetables, most of the herbs, and the chicken. Drizzle with the dressing and scatter with the remaining herbs and the peanuts, if using, to serve.

Nutrition per serving

Energy	243cal (1019kJ)
Carbohydrate	12g
of which sugar	11g
Fat	8.5g
of which saturated	1.5g
Sodium	1.4g
Fiber	4.5g

On the go

The chicken should be left to cool before packing, and kept in the fridge until lunchtime. Keep the dressing separate.

░░░░░░░░	Lettuce and herbs
▬▬▬▬▬▬	Tomatoes
//////////	Carrot, cucumber, and bell peppers
|||||||||	Chicken
～～～～～	Dressing

Smoked chicken salad *with papaya salsa*

With tropical fruits like papaya and mango now available all year round in most supermarkets, it has never been easier to bring a little bit of sunshine to your lunchtime, whatever the weather.

Serves 4   Prep 15 mins

Ingredients

salt and freshly ground
 black pepper

2 large handfuls of fresh
 spinach leaves

handful of fresh basil leaves

1lb (450g) smoked chicken,
 sliced

For the dressing

3 tbsp extra-virgin olive oil

1 tbsp white wine vinegar

1 tbsp mango juice

For the salsa

1 ripe fresh papaya

1 fresh red chile, seeded
 and finely chopped

juice of 1 lime

pinch of sugar

Method

1 First, make the dressing. Whisk together the oil, vinegar, and mango juice in a small bowl. Season well with salt and black pepper, and set aside.

2 Now make the salsa. Halve the papaya, and remove the seeds. Peel, then chop the flesh. In a bowl, toss together the papaya with the chile, lime juice, and sugar. Season to taste with the salt and black pepper.

3 In a large bowl, toss the spinach and basil with the dressing, then divide between 4 individual plates. Arrange the smoked chicken on top. Serve with the salsa spooned on top or on the side.

Nutrition per serving

Energy	280cals (1153kJ)
Carbohydrate	6g
of which sugar	6g
Fat	12.5g
of which saturated	2.5g
Sodium	0.2g
Fiber	2g

Tropical chicken salad *with curried yogurt*

Featuring fresh pineapple and mango, this is a protein-rich, fruity salad with a creamy, lightly curried dressing. It is low in saturated fat, and goes a long way to helping you reach your five a day.

Serves 4   Prep 10 mins

Ingredients

salt and freshly ground
    black pepper

12oz (350g) cooked skinless
    chicken, thickly shredded

1 small head crisp lettuce (such as
    iceberg or romaine), shredded

3 tbsp salted peanuts

3 tbsp cashew nuts

½ fresh pineapple, peeled,
    cored, and cut into segments

1 mango, pitted and cut
    into bite-sized pieces

For the dressing

3–4 tbsp Greek-style yogurt

pinch of mild curry powder
    (add more according to your
    liking), plus extra to garnish

juice of ½ lime

Method

1 First, make the dressing. Mix the ingredients together in a small bowl and season with salt and black pepper. Set aside.

2 Put the chicken, lettuce, and nuts in a large bowl and toss gently to combine. Drizzle with the dressing and toss again to coat.

3 When ready to serve, combine the pineapple and mango with the salad and add a pinch of black pepper. Transfer to a serving bowl and sprinkle over a little curry powder.

If you are on a calorie-controlled diet, you may wish to try a reduced-fat Greek yogurt in this recipe. This is usually a little thinner than full-fat yogurt, so you may need to use more for an effective dressing.

Nutrition per serving

Energy	312cals (1310kJ)
Carbohydrate	20g
of which sugar	18g
Fat	14g
of which saturated	3g
Sodium	0.2g
Fiber	3.5g

Antipasto salad

Combining lettuce varieties with spicy leaves really lifts this classic salad, but it is the inclusion of prosciutto that really makes it something special. Flavorful and delicate, you only need to add a few slices into the mix.

Serves 4   Prep 30 mins   Cook 10 mins

Ingredients

3½ cups green beans

sea salt and freshly ground black pepper

3 tbsp choppedparsley

2 tsp lemon thyme leaves

1 tbsp chopped fennel

2 tbsp extra-virgin olive oil

4½oz (125g) mixed lettuce and spicy salad leaves

1 × 14oz (400g) jar artichoke hearts

4 slices prosciutto

16 black olives, pitted and chopped

4½oz (125g) cherry tomatoes

2 scallions, chopped

3 tbsp chopped chervil

For the dressing

⅓ cup extra-virgin olive oil

½ garlic clove, crushed

1½ tbsp balsamic vinegar

Method

1 Bring a pot of lightly salted water to a boil. Trim off the ends of the green beans and blanch in the boiling water for 5–7 minutes. Refresh in cold water and drain.

2 Place the beans in a wide, shallow salad bowl. Season lightly with salt and pepper and sprinkle in half the parsley, lemon thyme, and fennel. Drizzle with the olive oil, toss, and set aside.

3 Make the dressing by pouring the olive oil into a small bowl. Season with salt and pepper, and then whisk in the garlic and balsamic vinegar.

4 Scatter the salad leaves over the beans, followed by the drained and halved artichoke hearts, thinly shredded prosciutto, olives, halved tomatoes, and scallions. Whisk the dressing again and drizzle it over the salad. Toss, sprinkle over the chervil, and serve.

Nutrition per serving	
Energy	259cals (1029kJ)
Carbohydrate	10g
of which sugar	9g
Fat	21g
of which saturated	3g
Sodium	0.4g
Fiber	6g

On the go

Prosciutto is thinly cut and quite delicate, so you should layer it near the top of the salad, beneath the salad leaves.

- Salad leaves and scallions
- Prosciutto
- Artichoke hearts and tomatoes
- Green beans and olives
- Dressing and herbs

Chorizo, chickpea, and mango salad

The one-pan cooking method used for this warm salad allows the chickpeas to take on the flavor of the rich, gently spiced chorizo. Make an extra batch and let it cool—it makes a hearty on-the-go lunch.

Serves 2   Prep 15 mins   Cook 15 mins

Ingredients

1 tbsp olive oil

5½oz (150g) chorizo, roughly chopped

1 × 14oz (400g) can chickpeas, drained and rinsed

3 cloves of garlic, finely chopped

handful of flat-leaf parsley, finely chopped

1 tbsp dry sherry

2 ripe mangoes, pitted and flesh diced

small handful of fresh basil leaves, roughly chopped

small handful of fresh mint leaves, roughly chopped

small handful of fresh cilantro, roughly chopped

9oz (250g) baby spinach leaves

Method

1 Heat the olive oil in a frying pan. Add the chorizo and chickpeas, cook over low heat for 1 minute, then add the garlic and parsley and cook for 1 more minute. Finally, add the sherry and cook for 10 minutes, stirring occasionally.

2 Put the mango and remaining herbs in a bowl and toss together, then add the chickpea mixture and combine well. Spoon onto the spinach leaves to serve.

If you prefer something even spicier, substitute chorizo with 12oz (350g) rotisserie chicken, roughly chopped into bite-sized pieces, and a dash of jerk seasoning.

Nutrition per serving

Energy	504cals (2106kJ)
Carbohydrate	31g
of which sugar	5.5g
Fat	24g
of which saturated	8g
Sodium	1.5g
Fiber	2.5g

On the go

If you don't want the mango to be stained by the chorizo, store the fruit in a separate container until lunchtime.

Spinach and herbs

Mango

Chickpea-chorizo mix

Bistro salad with frisée lettuce

Also known as a "salade lyonnaise," this is French comfort food at its finest. Master the timing of poaching the eggs, and you can be sure of a runny yolk waiting to ooze into the salad—perfect for dunking your croutons in.

Serves 4   Prep 5 mins   Cook 10 mins

Ingredients

4 eggs

1 tbsp lemon juice

olive oil

2 thick slices of bread, crusts removed and diced

1 garlic clove, halved

1 × ¼in (5mm) slice of fresh ginger (optional)

4oz (115g) smoked lardons

½–1 head frisée lettuce, torn

3 sprigs fresh thyme, leaves only

small handful of fresh flat-leaf parsley

small handful of fresh cilantro

1 small red onion, thinly sliced and separated into rings

For the dressing

2 tbsp red wine vinegar

¼ tsp red pepper flakes

2 tsp Worcestershire sauce

¼ tsp sugar

salt and freshly ground black pepper

Method

1 Poach the eggs in gently simmering water with the lemon juice for about 3 minutes. Scoop out and put straight into cold water.

2 Heat a little olive oil in a nonstick frying pan. Add the bread, garlic, and ginger, if using, toss and stir until golden. Drain on paper towel. Discard the garlic and ginger. In the same pan, dry-fry the lardons until crisp and golden. Drain on paper towels.

3 In a salad bowl, place the lettuce, and tear the herbs into it. Add the onion, lardons, and croutons. Add ⅓ cup olive oil to a pan with the dressing ingredients. Heat gently, stirring. Add to the salad, and toss. Divide between 4 bowls. Top each with a poached egg and serve immediately.

Nutrition per serving

Energy	396cals (1628kJ)
Carbohydrate	14g
of which sugar	3g
Fat	31g
of which saturated	6g
Sodium	1.5g
Fiber	1g

Prosciutto with pear and nectarine

Prosciutto is dry-cured rather than cooked, which helps to cultivate its nutty flavor. It is served here with sweet fruits and bitter endive, creating a salad full of the tastes of Italy.

Serves 4   Prep 15 mins

Ingredients

2–3 heads endive, leaves separated and rinsed

3 firm but ripe pears

3 firm but ripe nectarines

12 thin slices prosciutto

handful of almonds (skins on)

salt and freshly ground black pepper

crusty bread, to serve

For the dressing

⅓ cup extra-virgin olive oil

2 tbsp unsweetened apple juice

1 tbsp good-quality balsamic vinegar

Method

1 First, make the dressing. Put the oil, apple juice, and balsamic vinegar in a small bowl, and whisk together. Season well with salt and black pepper. Arrange the endive leaves in a single layer on a large serving plate, and drizzle with a little of the dressing.

2 Core and slice the pears, and halve, pit, and slice the nectarines. Arrange over the endive leaves along with the prosciutto, and toss together gently. Sprinkle over the almonds, then drizzle with a little more dressing. Season again, then serve immediately with some fresh crusty bread.

Nutrition per serving

Energy	337cals (1339kJ)
Carbohydrate	24g
of which sugar	23g
Fat	21g
of which saturated	4g
Sodium	1.5g
Fiber	5.5g

On the go

Pack a slice of fresh bread in a separate container, and you can use it to mop up any leftover dressing you have.

Almonds	
Parma ham	
Nectarines	
Pears	
Dressing	

Green papaya, beef, and noodle salad

A vibrant, Vietnamese-inspired noodle salad, this meal makes for a refreshing lunch. Green papayas are underripe fruit that feature in many Southeast Asian salads—if you can't find papaya, green mango works just as well.

Serves 4   Prep 20 mins, plus standing   Cook 8 mins

Ingredients

12oz (350g) fillet or flank steak

7oz (200g) rice vermicelli or mung bean noodles

1 medium green papaya or mango, peeled, seeded, and cut into matchsticks

¼ cup roasted unsalted peanuts, coarsely chopped

For the dressing

1 tsp lemongrass purée

1 tsp finely grated fresh ginger

2 tbsp chopped cilantro

2 tbsp Vietnamese nuoc mam or Thai fish sauce

2 tbsp chopped mint

juice of 2 limes

1 tsp brown sugar

2 fresh red chiles, seeded and finely chopped

Method

1 Preheat the broiler to high. Trim any fat from the steak and broil for 3–4 minutes on each side, or until browned but still pink in the center. Set aside for at least 15 minutes before slicing into thin strips.

2 Meanwhile, soak the vermicelli in boiling water until softened, or as directed on the package. Drain, rinse in cold water, then cut into manageable lengths with kitchen scissors. Set aside.

3 Mix together the lemongrass, ginger, cilantro, nuoc mam, mint, lime juice, sugar, and chiles.

4 Pile the noodles, papaya, and steak on a serving dish and add the dressing. Toss lightly together and scatter with peanuts before serving.

Nutrition per serving

Energy	437cals (1834kJ)
Carbohydrate	50g
of which sugar	7g
Fat	13g
of which saturated	4g
Sodium	2.1g
Fiber	2.5g

Nutty bresaola salad
with horseradish dressing

The sharpness of watercress is delicious with bresaola, a lean, air-dried salted beef from northern Italy. The citrus notes in the horseradish dressing beautifully round off this simple salad.

Serves 4   Prep 7 mins

Ingredients

2 bunches of really fresh watercress, stalks trimmed

8 slices bresaola or prosciutto

1 fennel bulb, trimmed and finely shredded

¼ cup walnuts, roughly chopped

For the dressing

3 tbsp extra-virgin olive oil

1 tbsp white wine vinegar

juice of 1 orange

1 tsp horseradish sauce (hot or cream)

salt and freshly ground black pepper

Method

1 First, make the dressing. Put all the ingredients in a small bowl and whisk until combined. Season well with salt and black pepper and set aside.

2 Scatter the watercress in a large, shallow serving bowl and top with the bresaola.

3 Add the fennel, toss to combine, and sprinkle over the walnuts. When ready to serve, drizzle with some of the dressing—you may not need it all.

You do not need to go to a delicatessen to source bresaola—most supermakets will stock this deli meat.

Nutrition per serving

Energy	140cals (569kJ)
Carbohydrate	1g
of which sugar	0.9g
Fat	11g
of which saturated	2g
Sodium	0.7g
Fiber	2g

On the go

For a larger lunch, add some more watercress and some diced red onion.

▨▨▨▨	Watercress
▧▧▧▧	Walnuts
‖‖‖‖‖	Bresaola
⋮⋮⋮⋮	Fennel
≈≈≈≈	Dressing

Pastrami and arugula salad *with olive salsa*

This is a sophisticated, minimalist salad, designed to accentuate the unmistakable flavor of pastrami with a salsa bursting with Italian flavors. Add a little spinach and a few tomatoes for a heartier meal.

Serves 2   Prep 15 mins

Ingredients

handful of fresh arugula

6oz (175g) thinly sliced pastrami or other cooked sliced beef

For the dressing

8–10 green olives, pitted and sliced

handful of plump dark raisins

2 tsp capers, rinsed and gently squeezed dry

drizzle of olive oil

small handful of fresh flat-leaf parsley, finely chopped

salt and freshly ground black pepper

Method

1 First, make the salsa. In a bowl, mix together the olives, raisins, capers, oil, and parsley. Taste, and season with a pinch of salt and some black pepper.

2 Arrange the arugula and pastrami or other sliced beef in a shallow serving bowl. Spoon over the salsa, and serve at room temperature.

Nutrition per serving

Energy	180cals (746kJ)
Carbohydrate	2g
of which sugar	1.5g
Fat	11g
of which saturated	2.5g
Sodium	2.5g
Fiber	1g

Thai-spiced lamb salad *with lime dressing*

The vibrant colors of this spicy lamb salad really sing out, making it perfect for a summer lunch. Be sure not to overcook the lamb, or slice into it without letting it rest first, or you'll risk losing those delicious meat juices.

Serves 4   Prep 10 mins   Cook 7–10 mins, plus resting

Ingredients

3 tbsp peanut oil

1lb 2oz (500g) boneless lamb leg or chump

3½oz (100g) Thai glass noodles, cooked

3 shallots, thinly sliced

handful of cilantro

12 Thai basil leaves

small handful of mint leaves

⅓ cup roasted peanuts, coarsely ground

For the dressing

grated zest and juice of 5 limes

3 tsp palm sugar or brown sugar

1 red chile, seeded and finely chopped

½ tsp Thai fish sauce

1 tsp tamarind

Nutrition per serving

Energy	391cals (1636kJ)
Carbohydrate	12g
of which sugar	5g
Fat	25g
of which saturated	7g
Sodium	0.6g
Fiber	1.6g

Method

1 For the dressing, place the lime zest and juice, sugar, chile, fish sauce, tamarind, and 1 tablespoon of peanut oil in a small bowl. Mix to combine all the ingredients and dissolve the sugar. Set aside.

2 Cut the lamb into eight equal strips. Heat a grill pan and add the remaining groundnut oil. Sear the lamb for about 2 minutes on each side. Do not overcook the lamb—it should be rare. Let rest for 3 minutes.

3 Slice the lamb thinly and place in a large bowl. Add the glass noodles, dressing, shallots, herbs, and peanuts, and toss to combine. Divide the salad between 4 individual plates and serve immediately.

Cheese

Soft and creamy or hard and crumbly, mildly
flavored or powerfully pungent—cheeses of all
textures and flavors feature in this diverse selection
of hearty, satisfying salad recipes.

Fava bean and feta panzanella bowl

Inspired by the classic Italian bread salad, this unique green version of panzanella is evocative of the fresh colors and flavors of spring, cut with the salty tang of crumbled feta.

Serves 4   Prep 25 mins, plus standing   Cook 10 mins

Ingredients

4 cups shelled fava beans

salt and freshly ground black pepper

5½oz (150g) ciabatta, diced into ¾in (2cm) cubes (about 3 cups)

¾ cup extra-virgin olive oil

2 tbsp white wine vinegar

1 large garlic clove, crushed

4 scallions, green parts removed and finely chopped

1⅓ cups feta cheese, roughly crumbled

handful of chopped mint leaves

2 tbsp chopped dill (optional)

4 handfuls of baby salad leaves

juice of 1 lemon

Method

1 Preheat the oven to 425°F (220°C). Cook the beans in boiling salted water for 2–3 minutes until just cooked, plunge them into cold water to cool them, and peel off the skins.

2 Meanwhile, toss the diced bread in ¼ cup of olive oil, sprinkle over a little salt and pepper, and place on a baking sheet. Cook at the top of the hot oven for about 8 minutes, turning once, until the bread is golden brown and crispy.

3 In a large serving bowl, whisk together the vinegar, garlic, and remaining olive oil, then season with plenty of pepper and just a little salt (as the feta is already salty). Add the fava beans, toasted bread, scallions, feta, and herbs, and toss well to coat.

4 Let the salad stand for 30 minutes to develop the flavors and soften the bread. Add the salad leaves and lemon juice, and serve.

Nutrition per serving

Energy	604cals (2431kJ)
Carbohydrate	25g
of which sugar	3g
Fat	46g
of which saturated	12g
Sodium	1.7g
Fiber	10g

On the go

Layer the beans between the bread and dressing to keep the bread dry and crispy, or simply store the dressing separately.

- Salad leaves
- Feta and scallions
- Toasted bread
- Fava beans
- Dressing and herbs

Green feta salad *with watercress mayonnaise*

Always buy the best-quality cheese you can find. Authentic feta is made entirely of sheep milk cheese, and must have been produced in Greece in order to receive the name—otherwise, it's just a poor-substitute hard cheese.

Serves 4   Prep 15 mins

Ingredients

salt and freshly ground black pepper

1 cup feta cheese, cut into cubes

1 cup fresh peas

2 handfuls of baby spinach leaves

small handful of fresh mint leaves

lemon wedges, to serve

For the dressing

handful of fresh watercress, roughly chopped

3–4 tbsp good-quality mayonnaise

1 tsp horseradish cream

Method

1 In a food processor, pulse the dressing ingredients together until well combined. Season with salt and pepper to taste.

2 Put the feta, peas, spinach, and mint in a bowl, and toss gently to mix. Season with a little pepper if you wish. Transfer to a serving bowl, and serve with the watercress mayonnaise and lemon wedges on the side.

If it's not the season for fresh peas, frozen ones make an ideal substitute. Leave them to defrost in a bowl, then pour over boiling water and let sit for about 5 minutes. Drain and refresh with fresh cold water.

Nutrition per serving

Energy	223cals (907kJ)
Carbohydrate	4.5g
of which sugar	2g
Fat	18g
of which saturated	7g
Sodium	1.2g
Fiber	2g

Watermelon and feta salad

This salad is a modern classic. The sweetness of the ripe melon contrasts wonderfully with the salty feta and the nuttiness of the pumpkin seeds—perfect for a refreshing summer lunch.

Serves 4   Prep 10 mins   Cook 5 mins

Ingredients

¼ cup pumpkin seeds

sea salt and freshly ground black pepper

¼ tsp chili powder

¼ cup olive oil

juice of 1 lemon

1lb 2oz (500g) watermelon, peeled, and cut into ¾in (2cm) cubes

½ red onion, thinly sliced

4 large handfuls of mixed salad leaves, such as watercress, arugula, or baby spinach

10oz (300g) feta cheese, cut into ½in (1cm) cubes

Method

1 Dry-fry the pumpkin seeds for 2–3 minutes until they start to pop. Add a pinch of sea salt and the chili powder, stir, and cook for 1 more minute. Set aside to cool.

2 In a large bowl, whisk together the oil, lemon juice, and sea salt and pepper to taste. Add the watermelon, red onion, and salad leaves, and toss well to coat with the dressing.

3 Scatter the feta and the seeds over the top of the salad, and serve immediately.

Nutrition per serving

Energy	419cals (1742kJ)
Carbohydrate	13g
of which sugar	11g
Fat	33g
of which saturated	13g
Sodium	2.8g
Fiber	1.8g

Rainbow wheat berry and feta salad

Despite what the name may suggest, wheat berries are not berries, but grains. They are whole kernels of wheat, with a creamy, nutty taste and a reddish-brown color—ideal for this bright, jewellike salad.

Serves 2   Prep 20 mins, plus overnight soaking and cooling   Cook 30 mins

Ingredients

¼ cup uncooked wheat berries

1 carrot, grated

1 zucchini, grated

⅓ cup pumpkin seeds

⅔ cup feta cheese, crumbled

2 tbsp chopped flat-leaf parsley

seeds of 1 small pomegranate

salt and freshly ground black pepper

juice of 1 lemon (optional)

Method

1 Place the wheat berries in a bowl, cover with water, and let soak overnight or for at least 8 hours. Then drain, rinse under running water, and drain well again.

2 Place the wheat berries in a lidded saucepan, cover with water, and bring to a boil, then reduce the heat to a simmer, and cover. Cook for 30 minutes, until tender. Remove from the heat, drain, and let cool completely.

3 Once cooled, place the wheat berries in a large bowl, along with the grated carrot and zucchini. Sprinkle over the pumpkin seeds and mix lightly to combine. Add the feta and parsley to the mixture and toss to combine.

4 Divide the salad equally between 2 salad bowls. Sprinkle over the pomegranate seeds and season to taste. Drizzle with lemon juice, if using, and serve immediately.

Nutrition per serving

Energy	399cals (1591kJ)
Carbohydrate	28g
of which sugar	10g
Fat	22g
of which saturated	9g
Sodium	1.3g
Fiber	6.5g

On the go

Create bold stripes of color by layering this salad, or toss it together for an all-in-one lunch dish.

Pomegranate and pumpkin seeds

Feta cheese

Carrot

Zucchini and parsley

Wheat berries and lemon juice

Greek olive salad
with herb vinaigrette

For this classic, deeply refreshing combination, choose tasty, pungent Kalamata olives and firm tomatoes, as well as an aromatic, strong extra-virgin olive oil for the vinaigrette.

Serves 6–8   Prep 25–30 mins, plus standing

Ingredients

salt and freshly ground
   black pepper

2 small cucumbers, peeled

2½lb (1kg) tomatoes

1 red onion, peeled and
   trimmed

2 green bell peppers, cored,
   seeded, and diced

4½oz (125g) Kalamata
   or other Greek olives

1 cup feta cheese, cut into
   cubes

For the dressing

½ cup extra-virgin
   olive oil

3 tbsp red wine vinegar

3–5 sprigs of mint, leaves
   picked and finely chopped

3–5 sprigs of oregano, leaves
   picked and finely chopped

7–10 sprigs of parsley, leaves
   picked and finely chopped

Method

1 To make the vinaigrette, gradually whisk the oil into the vinegar so that the mixture emulsifies and thickens slightly. Add the herbs, whisk again, and season to taste.

2 Cut each cucumber in half lengthwise. Scoop out the seeds with a teaspoon. Discard the seeds. Cut the cucumbers lengthwise into strips, then into ½in (1cm) slices.

3 Core the tomatoes, cut each into 8 wedges, then cut each wedge in half. Slice the onion into very thin rings, then gently separate the concentric circles within each ring.

4 Put the cucumbers, tomatoes, onion rings, and peppers in a large bowl. Briskly whisk the dressing and pour it over. Add the olives and feta, toss to coat, and season. Allow the flavors to mellow for about 30 minutes before serving.

Nutrition per serving	
Energy	211cals (883kJ)
Carbohydrate	7.5g
of which sugar	7g
Fat	17g
of which saturated	5g
Sodium	1g
Fiber	3.5g

On the go

With no toppings or salad leaves in this on-the-go salad, the feta cheese can be sprinkled into the container last.

‖‖‖‖‖‖‖‖‖	Feta cheese
≡≡≡≡≡	Cucumber and tomatoes
⧵⧵⧵⧵⧵	Peppers and onion
⋮⋮⋮⋮⋮	Olives
～～～～	Vinaigrette

Feta, spinach, and date salad

Sweet, chewy dates are an unusual salad ingredient, but when paired with salty feta and tangy preserved lemons, they make a wonderful Middle Eastern dish. They are also a great source of fiber, potassium, and iron.

Serves 2   Prep 10 mins

Ingredients

5½ oz (150g) baby spinach leaves

2 fresh dates, pitted and chopped

⅓ cup pine nuts, toasted

¾ cup reduced-fat feta cheese, crumbled or cut into small cubes

salt and freshly ground black pepper

2 preserved lemons, halved, pith removed, and skin finely chopped

For the dressing

1 tbsp olive oil

splash of white wine vinegar

½ tsp Dijon mustard

few stems of fresh dill, finely chopped

Method

1 First, make the dressing: whisk together the oil and vinegar and season with salt and black pepper, then stir in the mustard and the dill. Taste and adjust the seasoning as needed, then set aside.

2 Put the spinach leaves into a bowl and add the dates, pine nuts, and feta. Season, if desired. (If you are using a salty feta, you may not need to add salt.)

3 When ready to serve, whisk the dressing, pour into an empty salad bowl, and swirl until the dressing coats the bowl. Add the leaf and feta mixture and very gently toss with your hands to lightly coat the leaves. Sprinkle over the chopped lemon and serve.

Nutrition per serving	
Energy	352cals (1459kJ)
Carbohydrate	10g
of which sugar	10g
Fat	27g
of which saturated	5g
Sodium	1g
Fiber	3g

On the go

Toss the fresh dates in the dressing before packing them in the container to prevent the pieces from sticking together.

- Spinach
- Preserved lemons
- Feta and pine nuts
- Dates
- Dressing

Seared fig and halloumi salad

Halloumi only melts at a high temperature, making it the perfect component for a warm salad. Paired with figs and drizzled with a vinaigrette reduction, this dish would make a sophisticated starter for a dinner party.

Serves 4   Prep 10 mins   Cook 20 mins

Ingredients

10oz (300g) halloumi cheese, cut into ¼in (5mm) slices

8 large ripe figs, cut into quarters lengthwise

large handful of mixed salad leaves

¼ cup red wine vinegar

small handful of cilantro, finely chopped

1 red chile, seeded and finely chopped

1 garlic clove, crushed

olive oil, to serve

Method

1 Heat a large nonstick frying pan over medium heat. Add the halloumi and figs, and cook for 2–3 minutes on each side, until they start to brown. Once cooked, remove and place on a plate with the salad leaves.

2 Pour the red wine vinegar into the same pan and increase the heat slightly. Add the cilantro, chile, and garlic, and simmer over medium-high heat, until the sauce has reduced in volume by three-quarters.

3 Drizzle the dressing sparingly over the figs and cheese. Splash the salad with the oil and serve immediately.

Nutrition per serving

Energy	337cals (1291kJ)
Carbohydrate	17g
of which sugar	10g
Fat	22g
of which saturated	13g
Sodium	1.9g
Fiber	2.5g

Grilled halloumi and tomato salad

Simple and satisfying, this light salad makes halloumi cheese the star. If you find halloumi a little salty, you can soak it in buttermilk before grilling.

Serves 4   Prep 5 mins   Cook 15 mins

Ingredients

7oz (200g) cherry tomatoes, halved

3 tbsp olive oil

salt and freshly ground black pepper

9oz (250g) reduced-fat halloumi cheese, cut into ¼in (5mm) thick slices

3 garlic cloves, finely chopped

small handful of flat-leaf parsley, finely chopped

½ tsp paprika

small handful of basil, roughly chopped

9oz (250g) baby spinach leaves

Method

1 Preheat the oven to 350°F (180°C). Place the tomatoes in a roasting pan, drizzle with 1 tablespoon of the oil, and season with salt and pepper. Toss to coat, then, with the tomatoes sitting skin side down, roast in the oven for 15 minutes.

2 While the tomatoes are cooking, put the halloumi, garlic, parsley, paprika, and the remaining oil into a bowl and combine well. Heat a griddle pan until hot, then, after letting it drain first, carefully add a slice of halloumi to the pan. Repeat, adding the halloumi slices one by one until they are all in the griddle pan. When you have added the last one, go back to the first one and begin turning them over to cook on the other side. They should be golden brown. When you have turned them all, go back to the first one and begin removing them from the griddle pan.

3 Put the halloumi slices back into the bowl with the garlic, herb, and spice mix and stir gently. Add the cooked tomatoes to the mix along with the basil and stir to combine. Add the spinach leaves, toss together, and serve immediately.

Nutrition per serving

Energy	264cals (1105kJ)
Carbohydrate	3g
of which sugar	2g
Fat	19g
of which saturated	9g
Sodium	1.7g
Fiber	1.5g

Goat cheese stacks with toasted spelt

Stacked salads are a showstopping way to present a healthy meal. This recipe layers goat cheese and watermelon rounds with spelt, an ancient grain.

Makes 4 stacks   Prep 20 mins, plus overnight soaking   Cook 50 mins

Ingredients

¾ cup uncooked spelt, soaked

salt and freshly ground black pepper

1 tbsp olive oil

2 beef tomatoes, about 1¼lb (550g) in total, sliced into 8 rounds

8oz (225g) goat cheese, sliced into thin rounds

3lb 3oz (1½kg) watermelon, seeded and sliced into rounds

handful of basil leaves

a good drizzle of extra-virgin olive oil

Method

1 Place the spelt in a large bowl, cover with water, and let soak overnight or for about 8 hours. Then drain, rinse under running water, and drain well again.

2 Place the spelt in a lidded saucepan. Cover with 3 cups of water, add a pinch of salt, and bring to a boil. Then reduce the heat to a simmer and cover. Cook for about 40 minutes, until all the water has been absorbed. Remove from the heat and drain the remaining water. Heat the olive oil in a large nonstick frying pan over medium heat. Add the spelt and cook for about 10 minutes, stirring frequently, until golden brown. Remove from the heat and allow to cool.

3 To assemble the stacks, place a slice of tomato on each of 4 individual plates and season with salt and pepper. Top each one with a slice of goat's cheese, a slice of watermelon, and a few basil leaves. Repeat to get one more layer of each, then sprinkle over a few spoonfuls of the toasted spelt. Drizzle with the extra-virgin olive oil and season to taste. Serve immediately.

Nutrition per serving

Energy	533cals (2211kJ)
Carbohydrate	60g
of which sugar	30g
Fat	25g
of which saturated	12g
Sodium	0.9g
Fiber	2g

Caprese farro salad
with traditional pesto

Featuring fresh summer tomatoes, soft mozzarella, chewy farro grains, and a homemade pesto sauce, this colorful Italian salad makes a light yet satisfying lunch.

Serves 4   Prep 10 mins, plus cooling   Cook 50 mins

Ingredients

1 cup uncooked farro

8oz (225g) mozzarella cheese, diced

3 large tomatoes, cut into bite-sized pieces

For the dressing

1 cup basil, rinsed and dried, plus extra to garnish

2 tbsp pine nuts

1 garlic clove

2–3 tbsp extra-virgin olive oil

salt and freshly ground black pepper

Method

1 Rinse the farro under cold running water and place in a large saucepan. Cover with about 2½ cups of water and bring to a boil. Then reduce the heat to a simmer and cook, stirring occasionally, for about 40 minutes or until softened. Remove from the heat, drain, and set aside to cool.

2 To make the pesto, place the basil, pine nuts, garlic, and oil in a food processor and pulse until smooth. Season to taste, if needed.

3 Place the mozzarella and tomatoes in a large bowl. Add the pesto and cooled farro and stir to mix. Chill the salad in the fridge until ready to serve, garnished with a few basil leaves.

Nutrition per serving

Energy	459cals (1894kJ)
Carbohydrate	45g
of which sugar	4.5g
Fat	23g
of which saturated	9g
Sodium	0.6g
Fiber	2g

On the go

The bold layers of this salad mimic the stripes of the Italian flag. Use a clear glass jar to maximise the effect.

- Basil
- Mozzarella
- Tomato
- Farro
- Pesto

Tomato salad *with* *balsamic vinegarette*

Versatile and easy to prepare, this simple salad of tomatoes, red onion, and mozzarella bursts with vibrant colors and delicious Italian flavors.

Serves 4   Prep 10 mins

Ingredients

8 ripe plum tomatoes, sliced

6 cherry tomatoes, halved

1 small red onion, peeled and sliced

handful of fresh basil, torn

extra-virgin olive oil, to drizzle

salt and freshly ground black pepper

2 handfuls of arugula

balsamic vinegar, to drizzle

2 balls of reduced-fat mozzarella cheese, torn

Method

1 Place the tomatoes, onion, and half of the basil in a bowl. Drizzle with plenty of olive oil, season well, and toss to coat.

2 Arrange the arugula on a serving plate and drizzle with a little oil and some balsamic vinegar. Season and spoon the tomato and basil mixture on top. Add the torn mozzarella. Sprinkle over the remaining basil, and drizzle again with a little oil and balsamic vinegar. Serve immediately.

Nutrition per serving

Energy	159cals (664kJ)
Carbohydrate	9g
of which sugar	9g
Fat	12g
of which saturated	5.5g
Sodium	0.4g
Fiber	3g

Gorgonzola and ciabatta salad

Gorgonzola is a creamy blue-veined cheese made from unskimmed cow's milk. A little goes a long way in this panzanella-style Italian salad.

Serves 4   Prep 15 mins

Ingredients

3 slices ciabatta or other rustic country-style bread, toasted and cut into chunky, bite-sized cubes

2–3 tbsp olive oil

handful of basil, torn

salt and freshly ground black pepper

½ × 7oz (190g) jar roasted red peppers, drained and sliced

4 tomatoes, roughly chopped

handful of toasted pine nuts

2½oz (70g) gorgonzola or other mild blue cheese, cut into bite-sized cubes

Method

1 Put the bread cubes in a large bowl and drizzle with the olive oil. Add the basil, and season with salt and black pepper. Toss together, and let stand for about 10 minutes to develop the flavors.

2 Add the peppers, tomatoes, pine nuts, and cheese, and toss gently until everything is evenly mixed. Serve with cold cooked meats.

A cheese with a similar taste to gorgonzola is dolcelatte. Simply swap in 2 ½oz (75g) of the cheese.

Nutrition per serving

Energy	292cals (1209kJ)
Carbohydrate	15g
of which sugar	1g
Fat	21g
of which saturated	8g
Sodium	1.8g
Fiber	1g

On the go

Place the bread at the bottom of the container so that it can absorb the olive oil and tomato juices.

‖‖‖‖‖‖‖‖‖‖	Basil
∷∷∷∷∷∷	Pine nuts
▦▦▦▦	Tomatoes and peppers
≡≡≡≡	Blue cheese
⧄⧄⧄⧄	Ciabatta and olive oil

Celery and green apple salad *with* *blue cheese dressing*

In this salad, the strong tastes of celery and bitter leaves more than hold their own against the pungency of a blue cheese dressing, with the walnuts adding crunch and texture.

Serves 4   Prep 10 mins   Cook 2 mins

Ingredients

½ cup chopped walnuts

4 celery sticks, trimmed and sliced diagonally into ½in (1cm) slices

2 green apples, cored and cut into thin wedges

4 large handfuls of watercress or arugula

1¾oz (50g) blue cheese, to serve

For the dressing

10½oz (300g) blue cheese, plus extra for serving

¼ cup apple cider vinegar

¼ cup hazelnut or olive oil

salt and freshly ground black pepper

Method

1 In a frying pan or wok, dry-fry the walnuts for 2–3 minutes until they are golden and crispy, then set aside to cool.

2 To make the dressing, combine the blue cheese, vinegar, oil, and a good amount of black pepper in a food processor. Pulse the mixture until it is a smooth, creamy dressing that has a thick pouring consistency. Add up to 1 tbsp of cold water to thin the dressing a little, if it is too thick.

3 In a large bowl, mix the celery, apples, and watercress. Coat the salad with the dressing and check the seasoning. Top with the walnut pieces and blue cheese, crumbled or diced into bite-sized pieces.

Nutrition per serving

Energy	535cals (2190kJ)
Carbohydrate	9g
of which sugar	9g
Fat	47g
of which saturated	18g
Sodium	3.2g
Fiber	2.5g

On the go

Toss the apple in a little lemon juice before layering. You won't taste it, but it will preserve the color of the cut fruit while in the container.

Salad leaves

Walnuts

Blue cheese

Apple and celery

Blue cheese dressing

Wheat berries and roasted squash with blue cheese

A great dish for cool fall days, this warm salad is an excellent combination of sweet, roasted butternut squash and chewy wheat berries that are given an added salty element from the blue cheese.

Serves 4   *Prep 15 mins, plus overnight soaking and cooling*   *Cook 1 hr*

Ingredients

- 1¾ cups uncooked wheat berries
- 1¾lb (800g) butternut squash, seeded and cut into cubes
- 2 tbsp olive oil, plus extra for greasing
- salt and freshly ground black pepper
- 1 cup blue cheese, crumbled
- ½ cup balsamic vinegar

Method

1 Place the wheat berries in a large bowl, cover with water, and let soak overnight or for about 8 hours. Drain, rinse, and drain well again. Place in a large, lidded saucepan and cover with 4 cups of water. Bring to a boil, then reduce the heat and simmer, covered, for about 50 minutes. Remove from the heat, drain, and allow to cool slightly.

2 Meanwhile, preheat the oven to 400°F (200°C). Spread out the butternut squash on a greased baking sheet in an even layer, drizzle with oil, and season. Roast for 20 minutes, then remove from the oven, and stir to mix. Return the sheet to the oven and roast for 20 more minutes.

3 Place the wheat berries, squash, and cheese in a large bowl, drizzle with the balsamic vinegar, and toss to coat. Taste and adjust the seasoning, if needed, and serve.

Nutrition per serving

Energy	590cals (2452kJ)
Carbohydrate	83g
of which sugar	16g
Fat	21g
of which saturated	8.5g
Sodium	1.2g
Fiber	4g

On the go

Rinse the wheat berries under cold running water and drain well before layering in the container, so that the grains do not stick together.

- Blue cheese
- Butternut squash
- Wheat berries
- Balsamic vinegar

Goat cheese and beans *with chive dressing*

Different types of goat cheese, or chevre, have different textures, ranging from soft to firm. Semihard varieties are best for salads—not so soft that they cannot retain their shape, but still crumbly enough to scatter through the dish.

Serves 4   Prep 10 mins

Ingredients

1 × 14oz (400g) can lima beans, drained and rinsed

1 × 14oz (400g) can flageolet or navy beans, drained and rinsed

salt and freshly ground black pepper

1¾oz (50g) pea shoots

lemon juice, to taste

3½oz (100g) semihard goat cheese, broken up into pieces

extra-virgin olive oil, to drizzle

serrano ham, to serve (optional)

For the dressing

scant 1oz (25g) bunch of chives, finely chopped

2 tsp white wine vinegar

1 tbsp extra-virgin olive oil

1 tbsp fresh thyme

pinch of red pepper flakes

Method

1 First, make the dressing: combine the chives, vinegar, olive oil, thyme, and red pepper flakes in a large bowl and stir to combine. Add the lima and flageolet beans, season well with salt and pepper, and toss to coat.

2 Stir in the pea shoots, taste, and add a bit of lemon juice. Transfer to a shallow serving dish and top with the goat cheese, a drizzle of olive oil, and a bit of freshly ground black pepper. Serve with a little serrano ham on the side, if you wish.

Nutrition per serving

Energy	280cals (1170kJ)
Carbohydrate	30g
of which sugar	3g
Fat	11g
of which saturated	5g
Sodium	0.2g
Fiber	8.5g

On the go

If you want a more filling lunch, mix in some baby salad leaves with the pea shoots, such as spinach or lamb's lettuce.

Pea shoots

Serrano ham (optional)

Goat cheese

Mixed beans

Chive dressing

Marinated goat cheese salad

A glass jar of little goat cheeses, herbs, and chiles in oil is an eye-catcher in any kitchen. For the best flavor, marinate it a week in advance of serving.

Serves 8   Prep 20–25 mins, plus marinating   Cook 5–8 mins

Ingredients

4 small round semihard goat cheeses, each weighing about 2–3oz (60–90g)

2 bay leaves

2–3 sprigs of thyme

2–3 sprigs of rosemary

2–3 sprigs of oregano

2 small dried red chiles

2 tsp black peppercorns

2$^1/_2$ cups olive oil, plus more if needed

8 slices of whole-wheat bread, trimmed into rounds with a pastry cutter

2 heads endive, leaves separated

1 head butter leaf lettuce, leaves separated

For the dressing

2 tbsp red wine vinegar

1 tsp Dijon mustard

salt and freshly ground black pepper

2 tbsp chopped thyme

Method

1 Put the cheeses in a large glass jar with the herbs, chiles, and peppercorns. Add enough oil to cover generously. Seal the jar and let it marinade for at least 1 week.

2 Remove the cheeses from the marinade oil, draining off the excess. Strain the oil, setting aside at least ⅓ cup for the vinaigrette and a little more for the bread.

3 For the vinaigrette, combine the vinegar and mustard in a bowl. Gradually whisk in the reserved oil to emulsify the vinaigrette. Add the thyme and season to taste.

4 Preheat the oven to 400°F (200°C). Brush the bread rounds with a little of the strained oil and bake for 3–5 minutes, until lightly toasted. Heat the broiler. Cut each goat cheese in half horizontally and put a piece on top of each bread round. Broil for 2–3 minutes, until bubbling and golden.

5 Arrange the salad leaves on individual plates, drizzle with the vinaigrette, and place the cheese toasts on top.

Nutrition per serving

Energy	230cals (930kJ)
Carbohydrate	9g
of which sugar	1g
Fat	16.5g
of which saturated	8g
Sodium	0.8g
Fiber	2g

Nutty goat cheese and beet salad

Cooked beets add a healthy, colorful boost to any salad. Make sure to avoid pickled beets, as they would overpower the other flavors in the dish.

Serves 4   Prep 15 mins

Ingredients

2 handfuls of arugula

4–6 large ready-cooked beets, roughly chopped

6oz (175g) semihard goat cheese, sliced

handful of shelled pistachios, roughly chopped

For the dressing

3 tbsp extra-virgin olive oil

1 tbsp white wine vinegar

2 shallots, finely chopped

1 tsp whole-grain mustard

pinch of sugar

salt and freshly ground black pepper

Method

1 To make the dressing, place the oil, vinegar, and shallots in a small bowl, and whisk together thoroughly. Add the mustard and sugar, and season well with salt and black pepper. Whisk again, then taste. Season again as needed—but remember to let the dressing stand for a while first, to develop the flavors.

2 Arrange the arugula on a large serving plate or 4 individual plates, then top with the beets and goat cheese. Drizzle with a little of the dressing, then sprinkle over the pistachios. Add more dressing, if you wish.

Nutrition per serving

Energy	304cals (1261kJ)
Carbohydrate	10g
of which sugar	9g
Fat	23g
of which saturated	9g
Sodium	0.9g
Fiber	3g

On the go

Be aware that the beets may stain the goat cheese layer red. If you would like to avoid this, keep the beets in a separate container.

Pistachios

Arugula

Goat cheese

Beets

Dressing

Grains and pulses

Good things come in small packages, and that is
certainly true in this chapter. Each tiny grain, bean,
and lentil is bursting with nutritional goodness, from
protein-rich ancient grains like freekeh and millet to
the humble chickpea, packed with fiber, iron, and zinc.

Jeweled couscous and apricot salad

This simple yet stunning Middle Eastern salad needs no cooking at all. Dotted with pomegranate seeds and chewy dried apricots, it makes a wonderful sharing dish for a dinner party.

Serves 6   Prep 12 mins, plus cooling

Ingredients

1¾ cups couscous

1½ tbsp olive oil

hot vegetable stock, to cover

⅓ cup pine nuts

¾ cup dried apricots, finely chopped

large handful of cilantro, finely chopped

¼ cup extra-virgin olive oil

juice of 1 large lemon

salt and freshly ground black pepper

2–3 tbsp pomegranate seeds, to serve

Method

1 Put the couscous in a bowl and drizzle with olive oil. Pour over the hot vegetable stock and stir briefly, so that the liquid just covers the couscous. Cover the bowl with plastic wrap and set aside for 5 mintues.

2 Test the grains: they should be nearly soft, with all the water soaked in. Fork over the couscous and allow it to cool, fluffing it up occasionally to separate the grains.

3 Meanwhile, dry-fry the pine nuts in a nonstick frying pan over medium heat, stirring, until they are golden brown. Be careful, as they can burn quickly. Set aside to cool.

4 Toss together the cooled couscous, pine nuts, apricots, and cilantro. Mix in the olive oil and lemon juice, then season to taste. Scatter over the pomegranate seeds and serve.

Nutrition per serving

Energy	396cals (1657kJ)
Carbohydrate	46g
of which sugar	9g
Fat	18g
of which saturated	2g
Sodium	0.7g
Fiber	4g

On the go

Couscous can be filling, so take care not to overfill your container. If you do make too much, it will keep for up to 3 days in the fridge.

Cilantro

Pomegranate seeds

Pine nuts and dried apricots

Couscous

Extra-virgin olive oil and lemon juice

Couscous with pine nuts and almonds

This dish makes tasty alternative to rice, and is a low-fat source of protein. It can be enjoyed hot or cold, making it the perfect candidate for both evening meals and speedy leftover lunches.

Serves 4   Prep 15 mins, plus standing

Ingredients

1 cup couscous

hot vegetable stock, to cover

1 red bell pepper, seeded and chopped

½ cucumber, seeded and diced

½ cup raisins

¾ cup dried apricots, chopped

12 black olives, pitted

½ cup blanched almonds, lightly toasted

½ cup pine nuts, lightly toasted

¼ cup light olive oil

juice of ½ lemon

1 tbsp chopped mint leaves

salt and freshly ground black pepper

Method

1 Put the couscous in a bowl and pour over enough hot vegetable stock to cover. Seal with plastic wrap and let sit for 5 minutes, or until the couscous has absorbed all the water, then fluff up the grains lightly with a fork.

2 Stir in the bell pepper, cucumber, raisins, apricots, olives, almonds, and pine nuts.

3 Whisk together the olive oil, lemon juice, and mint. Season to taste with salt and pepper and stir into the couscous. Serve at once while warm, or allow to cool.

Nutrition per serving	
Energy	619cals (2590kJ)
Carbohydrate	63g
of which sugar	31g
Fat	33g
of which saturated	3g
Sodium	0.3g
Fiber	7g

On the go

Don't pack the couscous in too tightly. Scatter the fluffy grains on the dressing so it can absorb the flavors of the liquid.

(pattern)	Dried fruit and nuts
(pattern)	Olives
(pattern)	Peppers and cucumber
(pattern)	Couscous
(pattern)	Olive oil, lemon juice, and mint

Moroccan couscous salad

Quick and simple, this delicious salad is full of fiber, low in fat, and makes a satisfying midweek meal. To add a little more color, fry a few chopped peppers along with the zucchini.

Serves 4   Prep 10 mins   Cook 10 mins

Ingredients

1½ cups couscous

hot vegetable stock, to cover

olive oil, for frying

2 zucchini, chopped

good pinch of paprika

juice of 2 lemons

handful of flat-leaf parsley, finely chopped

handful of olives, pitted and chopped

salt and freshly ground black pepper

Method

1 Place the couscous in a large bowl and pour over just enough hot vegetable stock to cover. Seal with plastic wrap and let sit for 5 minutes, or until the couscous has absorbed all the water, then fluff the grains up lightly with a fork.

2 Heat a little olive oil in a frying pan and cook the zucchini until golden. Add to the couscous, paprika, lemon juice, parsley, and olives.

3 Season well and stir to combine. Serve immediately, or allow to cool.

Nutrition per serving

Energy	215cals (898kJ)
Carbohydrate	32g
of which sugar	1g
Fat	7g
of which saturated	1g
Sodium	0.6g
Fiber	1g

On the go

To minimize condensation, blot the fried zucchini with a paper towel and allow to cool before adding it to the salad container.

- Parsley
- Olives
- Zucchini
- Couscous
- Lemon juice and paprika

Millet and sweet corn with roasted leeks

Packed with plenty of peppers and chiles, this fiery millet salad mix is certainly memorable—not least of which is its presentation on a bed of leeks.

Serves 6   *Prep 15 mins, plus soaking and cooling*   *Cook 40 mins*

Ingredients

¼ cup olive oil

½ cup uncooked millet

salt and freshly ground black pepper

1 small red onion, diced

2 red bell peppers, seeded and diced

3 cups fresh sweet corn kernels

1 jalapeño, diced

2 large poblano chiles, roasted (see p15) and sliced

½ tbsp cayenne pepper

½ tsp smoked paprika

3 scallions, thinly sliced

½ cup plain yogurt

juice of 1 lime

6 leeks, trimmed, cleaned, and halved lengthwise

Method

1 Heat 1 tablespoon of the oil in a large, lidded saucepan over medium heat. Add the millet and cook for 2–3 minutes, stirring frequently. Add 2 cups of water, season, and bring to a boil. Reduce the heat, cover, and simmer for 15 minutes. Remove from the heat and set aside, covered, for 10 minutes, then fluff up the grains with a fork. Allow to cool.

2 Meanwhile, heat 1 tablespoon of the oil in a frying pan over medium heat. Fry the onion and bell peppers, season, and cook for 5 minutes. Add the sweet corn, jalapeño, chiles, and spices. Cook for 5–10 minutes, stirring occasionally.

3 Reduce the heat and add the scallions and yogurt. Cook for about 2 minutes, stirring, until the yogurt has melted. Add the lime juice and season. Transfer the mixture to a large bowl, add the millet, and stir to combine. Set aside.

4 Set the broiler to medium. Coat the leeks in the remaining oil and season well. Broil the leeks for 20 minutes, turning frequently. Transfer to a plate, cover with foil, and let sit for 5 minutes to steam. Place on 6 individual plates, spoon over the millet mix, and serve.

Nutrition per serving

Energy	247cals (970kJ)
Carbohydrate	27g
of which sugar	9g
Fat	10g
of which saturated	2g
Sodium	0.1g
Fiber	7g

Bulgur wheat with mixed peppers and goat cheese

Sweet, crunchy bell peppers and creamy goat cheese are a winning combination. Bulgur wheat is a great staple for your pantry—it's a source of fiber and protein, and very easy to prepare.

Serves 4   Prep 15 mins

Ingredients

1¾ cups fine bulgur wheat

1¼ cups hot vegetable stock

salt and freshly ground black pepper

1 bunch of scallions, finely chopped

1 orange bell pepper, seeded and diced

1 yellow bell pepper, seeded and diced

pinch of mild paprika

handful of fresh mint leaves, finely chopped

juice of 1 lemon

½ cup soft goat cheese, crumbled

extra-virgin olive oil, for drizzling

Method

1 Put the bulgur wheat in a large bowl, and pour over enough stock to just cover the bulgur. Let stand for 10 minutes, then stir with a fork to fluff up the grains. Season with salt and pepper to taste.

2 Add the scallions, orange and yellow bell peppers, paprika, mint, and lemon juice, and stir well. Taste, and season again, if needed. To serve, top with the goat cheese and a generous drizzle of olive oil.

Nutrition per serving

Energy	422cals (1698kJ)
Carbohydrate	53g
of which sugar	7g
Fat	15g
of which saturated	6.5g
Sodium	0.9g
Fiber	7g

On the go

Soft goat cheese may crumble during transit, so you could use a semihard variety for this on-the-go salad instead.

Scallions

Goat cheese

Peppers

Bulgur wheat

Olive oil, lemon juice, paprika, and mint

Bulgur, eggplant, and pomegranate seed salad

This superfood salad has everything you need to power you through your day, including magnesium from the bulgur wheat, fiber and B-vitamins from the eggplant, and an antioxidant boost from the pomegranate seeds.

Serves 5   Prep 5 mins   Cook 25 mins

Ingredients

2 tbsp olive oil

2 eggplants, chopped into bite-sized pieces

pinch of paprika

2 cups bulgur wheat

1¼ cups hot vegetable stock

salt and freshly ground black pepper

½ cup hazelnuts, toasted

½ cup pomegranate seeds

Method

1 Put 1 tablespoon of the oil in a large frying pan set over low heat, and toss the eggplant pieces in the oil. Cook on medium-high heat for 10–15 minutes, or until the eggplant starts to turn golden, adding the remaining oil, if needed (as the eggplant may soak it up quickly). Add the paprika, toss, and cook for a few more minutes. Remove from the heat and set aside.

2 Put the bulgur wheat into a large bowl and pour the stock over it so that it is just covered. Cover with plastic wrap and let sit for 8–10 minutes, then fluff up with a fork to separate the grains.

3 Stir the bulgur wheat into the pan with the eggplant and mix well. Taste and season as required. Stir in the hazelnuts and sprinkle over the pomegranate seeds.

Nutrition per serving

Energy	454cals (1891kJ)
Carbohydrate	59g
of which sugar	5g
Fat	20g
of which saturated	2g
Sodium	0.4g
Fiber	4g

On the go

Ensure everything is completely cool before adding to the container. Set the eggplant on paper towels to reduce excess moisture.

- Pomegranate seeds
- Hazelnuts
- Eggplant
- Bulgur wheat

Rustic tabbouleh

Tabbouleh is a wonderful Middle Eastern dish of bulgur wheat, tomatoes, onions, and plenty of parsley. Enjoy with some warm pita bread for a satisfying dinner, or pack it up for lunch with crisp spears of romaine lettuce.

Serves 6   Prep 15 mins

Ingredients

¾ cup fine bulgur wheat

¼ cup extra-virgin olive oil

1 cup hot water

2 large tomatoes, cored, seeded, and finely chopped

½ small red onion, finely chopped

½ cucumber, peeled, seeded, and finely chopped

4 scallions, thinly sliced

3 bunches of curly parsley, finely chopped

¼ cup finely chopped mint leaves

juice of 2 lemons

sea salt and freshly ground black pepper

romaine lettuce and pita bread, to serve (optional)

Method

1 Rinse the bulgur wheat. Add to a medium bowl with 1 tablespoon of the extra-virgin olive oil, cover with near-boiling water, and stir. Let it stand for 15 minutes, then strain in a fine-mesh sieve, pressing gently to remove all the liquid. Fluff with a fork.

2 In a large bowl, toss the bulgur with the tomatoes, red onion, cucumber, scallions, parsley, mint, lemon juice, and the remaining extra-virgin olive oil. Season to taste, cover, and set aside for 1 hour to develop the flavors.

3 Serve at room temperature or cold with lettuce and pita bread, if you like. Tabbouleh keeps in the fridge for 3 days.

Tabbouleh is traditionally made with curly parsley. Flat-leaf parsley won't provide the same slightly chewy consistency or intensity of flavor.

Nutrition per serving

Energy	151cals (605kJ)
Carbohydrate	16g
of which sugar	3.5g
Fat	8g
of which saturated	1g
Sodium	0.8g
Fiber	2.5g

On the go

Make this a lunch to really savor: pack some pita bread, or even some cacık (see p104) in its own container.

Romaine lettuce (optional)

Scallions and herbs

Cucumber

Tomatoes and red onion

Bulgur wheat, lemon juice, and olive oil

Avocado, cilantro, and lime tabbouleh

The inclusion of lime and avocado in this tabbouleh gives a modern twist to a classic dish. The lime juice naturally preserves the avocado, keeping it fresh and appetizing while the flavors combine in the fridge.

Serves 4   Prep 15 mins, plus soaking and chilling

Ingredients

1¼ cups bulgur wheat

salt and freshly ground black pepper

2 tomatoes, diced

1 avocado, peeled, pitted, and diced

1 small red bell pepper, seeded and diced

⅓ cup red onion, diced

handful of cilantro, roughly chopped

½ cup lime juice

2 tbsp extra-virgin olive oil

Method

1 Place 1½ cups of water in a small saucepan and bring to a boil. Place the bulgur wheat and a large pinch of salt in a large bowl. Pour the boiling water into the bowl, cover, and allow to soak for about 30 minutes.

2 Drain any excess water from the bulgur wheat and place it in a large bowl. Then add the tomatoes, avocado, bell pepper, onion, and cilantro. Mix well to combine. Transfer the mixture to a large serving bowl.

3 Drizzle the lime juice and oil over the mixture. Toss well to coat. Season to taste with salt and black pepper, if needed. Mix well and chill the tabbouleh in the fridge for about 20 minutes before serving.

Nutrition per serving

Energy	306cals (1275kJ)
Carbohydrate	38g
of which sugar	5g
Fat	14g
of which saturated	2.5g
Sodium	1.9g
Fiber	2.4g

On the go

Toss the avocado in the lime juice before layering. The juice will soak into the bulgur while keeping the avocado green.

Red onion

Tomato and bell pepper

Avocado and lime juice

Bulgur wheat, cilantro, and olive oil

Tabbouleh *with cacık*

This tabbouleh recipe features cacık, a traditional yogurt dip flavored with cucumber, garlic, and herbs. It is similar to Greek tzatziki, and pairs well with any Middle Eastern salad dish.

Serves 4   Prep 30–35 mins, plus soaking and chilling

Ingredients

¾ cup bulgur wheat

salt and freshly ground
  black pepper

9oz (250g) tomatoes, peeled,
  seeded, and chopped

2 scallions, trimmed
  and chopped

small bunch of curly parsley,
  chopped

3 tbsp lemon juice

¼ cup olive oil

small bunch of mint, chopped

3–4 pita breads, to serve

For the dressing

1 small cucumber

1 large garlic clove, finely
  chopped

¼ tsp ground coriander

¼ tsp ground cumin

1 cup natural yogurt

Nutrition per serving

Energy	436cals (1833kJ)
Carbohydrate	63g
of which sugar	10g
Fat	14.5g
of which saturated	3g
Sodium	0.9g
Fiber	3g

Method

1 Put the bulgur wheat in a large bowl and pour over enough cold water to cover generously. Let it soak for 30 minutes, then drain through a sieve and squeeze out any remaining water with your fist.

2 Meanwhile, prepare the cucumber for the cacıc: trim the ends, cut in half lengthwise, and scoop out the seeds with a teaspoon. Dice the cucumber halves, put in a colander, sprinkle over salt, and stir to mix. Let sit for 15–20 minutes to draw out the bitter juices, then rinse under cold running water and drain.

3 For the tabbouleh, in a large bowl, combine the bulgur, tomatoes, scallions, parsley, lemon juice, oil, two-thirds of the mint, and plenty of salt and pepper. Mix and taste for seasoning, then cover and chill in the fridge for at least 2 hours.

4 To make the cacık, put the preparedcucumber in a bowl and add the garlic, remaining mint, ground coriander, ground cumin, and salt and pepper. Pour in the yogurt. Stir to combine and taste for seasoning. Chill in the fridge for at least 2 hours, to blend the flavors.

5 Warm the pita breads in a low oven for 3–5 minutes, then remove and cut into strips. Take the salad and cacık out of the fridge and allow it to come to room temperature. Divide it into 4 servings with warm slices of pita bread alongside them.

Herb tabbouleh *with pomegranate molasses*

A fruity dressing adds a delightful lift to any salad. This recipe features pomegranate molasses, a concentrated syrup that adds a luxurious sweetness to any Middle Eastern dish.

Serves 4   Prep 25 mins

Ingredients

For the salad

salt and freshly ground
  black pepper

½ cup fine bulgur wheat

6 tbsp chopped flat-leaf parsley

1 tbsp finely chopped mint leaves

1 tbsp chopped cilantro

4 scallions, finely chopped

4 cherry tomatoes, chopped

For the dressing

1 garlic clove, crushed

½ tsp five-spice powder

1 tbsp lemon juice

1 tsp finely grated lemon zest

1 tbsp pomegranate molasses

¼ cup extra-virgin olive oil

Method

1 To make the dressing, combine the garlic, a little salt, the five-spice powder, the lemon juice and zest, and the pomegranate molasses in a bowl. Whisk in the olive oil and season with salt and pepper to taste. Let stand while you prepare the ingredients for the salad.

2 Put the bulgur in a shallow bowl, cover with boiling water, and allow to swell for 2 minutes. Place into a sieve, drain, and refresh with plenty of cold water. Fluff up the bulgur with a fork, then shake and drain it well.

3 Put the bulgur into the bowl with the dressing mixture. Add the parsley, mint, cilantro, scallions, and tomatoes. Toss just to coat and season again with salt and pepper just before serving.

Nutrition per serving

Energy	151cals (605kJ)
Carbohydrate	16g
of which sugar	3.5g
Fat	8g
of which saturated	1g
Sodium	0.8g
Fiber	2.5g

On the go

The bulgur will steep in the pomegranate dressing while in the container, enriching the grains with fruity sweetness.

- Herbs
- Scallions
- Tomatoes
- Bulgur wheat
- Pomegranate molasses dressing

Chickpea, bulgur, and cranberry salad

This is a hearty and filling salad with nuts, fruits, and grains. Canned chickpeas do not require soaking, as they soften in the water they are stored in. As a result, they make the perfect salad ingredient when time is short.

Serves 4   Prep 10 mins

Ingredients

1 cup bulgur wheat

salt and freshly ground black pepper

1 × 14oz (400g) can chickpeas, drained and rinsed

1 sweet crisp apple, cored and diced

handful of walnuts, roughly chopped

¼ cup dried cranberries

juice of 1 lemon

½ tsp paprika

2–3 tbsp olive oil

Method

1 Put the bulgur wheat in a bowl and pour over enough hot water to cover. Set aside and let stand for about 10 minutes, then fluff up the grains with a fork. Season with salt and pepper to taste.

2 Put the chickpeas in another bowl, then add the apple, walnuts, and cranberries, and stir to combine.

3 Add the bulgur wheat and lemon juice, sprinkle over the paprika, and stir. Drizzle with a little olive oil and serve.

If you have time, you can gently warm the chickpeas in a saucepan while still in their water. This softens them even more and helps to bring out their flavor.

Nutrition per serving

Energy	331cals (1379kJ)
Carbohydrate	40g
of which sugar	4g
Fat	11g
of which saturated	1g
Sodium	trace
Fiber	5g

On the go

In addition to preserving the cut apple, the lemon juice and paprika will trickle down into the bulgur and chickpeas, flavoring them.

Cranberries

Walnuts

Apple, lemon juice, and paprika

Bulgur wheat

Chickpeas

Freekeh sweet and spicy warm salad

This warming and colorful salad combines freekeh, an ancient Middle Eastern grain, with spiced roasted squash and sweet, sticky dates, making it an utterly divine dinner idea for cold winter evenings.

Serves 4   Prep 15 mins, plus cooling   Cook 40 mins

Ingredients

2 tsp ground cinnamon

1 tsp grated ginger

1 tsp ground cumin

2 tbsp light olive oil

1 butternut squash, seeded and cut into ¾in (2cm) cubes

1 cup cracked freekeh

1 small head radicchio, roughly chopped

8 dried pitted dates, about 1½oz (40g) in total, roughly chopped

¼ cup roughly chopped flat-leaf parsley, to serve

For the dressing

¼ cup extra-virgin olive oil

juice of 1 lemon

1 tbsp honey

salt and freshly ground black pepper

Method

1 Preheat the oven to 400°F (200°C). Combine the spices and olive oil in a small bowl. Place the butternut squash on a baking sheet and coat with the spice mixture. Bake for 30–35 minutes, or until the squash is tender.

2 Meanwhile, rinse the freekeh and place in a large saucepan. Cover with 3½ cups of water and bring to a boil. Reduce the heat to a simmer and cook for 15 minutes, or until almost all the water has been absorbed. Remove from the heat, drain any remaining water, and allow to cool slightly.

3 For the dressing, place all the ingredients in a bowl. Season to taste and whisk to combine. Place the radicchio and dates in a large serving dish. Add the squash and freekeh, pour over the dressing, season to taste, and toss until well combined. Serve warm, garnished with parsley.

Nutrition per serving	
Energy	456cals (1808kJ)
Carbohydrate	55g
of which sugar	20g
Fat	19g
of which saturated	2.5g
Sodium	0.2g
Fiber	11.5g

On the go

Allow all the separate components of this salad to cool completely before layering them in a container.

Radicchio

Dates

Spiced squash

Freekeh

Dressing and parsley

Quinoa and mango with toasted coconut

This healthy salad is full of big, tropical flavors and bright colors. Toasted coconut is a delightfully unusual salad topping; try scattering a few over any grain-based salad for added crunch.

Serves 4   Prep 15 mins   Cook 10 mins

Ingredients

1¾oz (50g) unsweetened or flaked coconut

salt and freshly ground black pepper

1¾ cups uncooked quinoa

1 × 14oz (400g) can lima beans, drained and rinsed

½ red onion, finely chopped

1 large mango, peeled, pitted, and cut into bite-sized pieces

1 lime, peeled, segmented, and segments halved

handful of mint leaves, finely chopped

handful of flat-leaf parsley, finely chopped

For the dressing

3 tbsp olive oil

1 tbsp white wine vinegar

pinch of sugar

Method

1 Toast the coconut by dry-frying it in a pan over medium heat for 2–3 minutes until golden, stirring so that it doesn't burn. Remove from the heat and set aside to cool.

2 To make the dressing, place all the ingredients in a small bowl and whisk. Taste and adjust the seasoning as needed.

3 Rinse the quinoa under running water, drain, and place in a lidded saucepan. Add enough water to cover, bring to a boil, and cook for 15–20 minutes or until almost all the water is absorbed. Remove from the heat, drain well, and pour into a large serving bowl.

4 While the quinoa is still warm, stir in the lima beans, onion, mango, lime, mint, and parsley, and season. Pour over the dressing and stir well. Sprinkle over the toasted coconut and serve immediately.

Nutrition per serving

Energy	460cals (1935kJ)
Carbohydrate	54g
of which sugar	12.5g
Fat	20g
of which saturated	8g
Sodium	0.8g
Fiber	7.5g

Quinoa, fennel, and pomegranate salad

The peppery and licorice notes of fennel contrast well with the nutty quinoa and the sweet pomegranate seeds in this decadent salad bowl.

Serves 4   Prep 10 mins, plus standing   Cook 15 mins

Ingredients

1 cup uncooked quinoa

1½ cups vegetable stock

1 tsp ground cumin

1 fennel bulb

3 tbsp olive oil

1 tbsp lemon juice

salt and freshly ground
   black pepper

4 scallions, trimmed
   and thinly sliced

3 tbsp chopped cilantro

2 tbsp chopped mint

¾ cup pomegranate seeds

Method

1 Rinse the quinoa under cold running water. Drain and place in a large, lidded saucepan. Add the stock and cumin and bring to a boil, stirring frequently. Cover and cook over medium heat for about 10 minutes. Remove from the heat, drain, cover, and set aside for 10 minutes to fluff up.

2 To prepare the fennel, trim the stalks, root end, and any tough outer pieces from the bulb and reserve the fronds. Cut the bulb in half and then into thin slices lengthwise.

3 Heat 2 tablespoons of the oil in a large frying pan over medium heat. Add the fennel and cook for about 5 minutes, turning once, until golden. Transfer to a bowl and toss with the lemon juice, remaining oil, and seasoning.

4 Add the scallions, herbs, and fennel fronds to the bowl. Then add the quinoa and half of the pomegranate seeds. Stir to mix, then season, if needed. Divide the salad between 4 individual bowls, sprinkle over the remaining seeds, and serve.

Nutrition per serving

Energy	525cals (2197kJ)
Carbohydrate	28g
of which sugar	7.5g
Fat	11g
of which saturated	1.5g
Sodium	0.8g
Fiber	7g

On the go

Remove excess frying oil from the fennel with a paper towel and allow to cool before layering, so that it remains crisp in the container.

Herbs and fennel fronds

Pomegranate seeds

Fennel and scallions

Quinoa

Lemon juice and olive oil

Mexican quinoa and kidney bean salad

This fun salad packs a real punch of flavor and texture. Great for kids and grown-ups alike, it makes an easily portable lunch—just take a bag of tortilla chips with you alongside the salad container.

Serves 2   Prep 10–15 mins, plus cooling   Cook 20 mins

Ingredients

⅓ cup uncooked quinoa

1 × 14oz (400g) can red kidney beans, drained

⅓ cup sweet corn

½ red onion, finely chopped

1 red bell pepper, seeded and finely chopped

4–6 slices pickled jalapeños, finely chopped

1 avocado, pitted and cut into cubes

1 head romaine lettuce

1¾oz (50g) plain corn tortilla chips, crumbled, plus extra to serve

1 lime, halved, to serve

Method

1 Rinse the quinoa under running water, drain, and place in a lidded saucepan. Add 1 cup of water to cover and bring to a boil. Reduce the heat to a simmer, cover, and cook for 15–20 minutes or until almost all of the liquid has been absorbed and the quinoa is fluffy. Remove from the heat, drain any remaining water, and set aside to cool.

2 Mix together the quinoa, kidney beans, sweet corn, onion, bell pepper, and jalapeños in a large bowl. Then add the avocado and mix lightly to combine.

3 Roughly shred the lettuce and add to the bowl. Sprinkle the crumbled tortilla chips over the mixture and toss lightly. Transfer the salad to a serving plate. Serve with tortilla chips and lime halves to squeeze over the salad.

Nutrition per serving

Energy	555cals (2322kJ)
Carbohydrate	57g
of which sugar	10g
Fat	24g
of which saturated	4g
Sodium	0.5g
Fiber	20g

On the go

Instead of packing a whole lime half with your portable meal, squeeze the juice over the avocado before layering the salad, to avoid discoloration.

Romaine lettuce

Avocado, lime juice, and jalapeños

Sweet corn, onion, and bell pepper

Quinoa

Kidney beans

Tortilla chips

Lentil salad with lemon and almonds

The crisp taste of French green lentils is enhanced in this salad by the mellow taste of preserved lemon, a refreshing Middle Eastern delicacy that can be found in most supermarkets.

Serves 6   Prep 10 mins, plus standing   Cook 15–20 mins

Ingredients

2 cups French green lentils

2 preserved lemons, rinsed and diced small

2 tbsp chopped cilantro

2 scallions, thinly sliced

3 tbsp red wine vinegar

½ cup extra-virgin olive oil

salt and freshly ground black pepper

¼ cup sliced almonds, toasted

cilantro leaves

Method

1 Bring a large pot of water to a boil and add the lentils. Return to a boil, reduce the heat, cover, and simmer for 15–20 minutes, or until the lentils are just tender. Drain, then rinse quickly in cold water and drain well.

2 Place the lentils in a large bowl and stir in the lemons, chopped cilantro, and half of the scallions. In a separate bowl, whisk together the vinegar and oil, season to taste with salt and pepper, and combine with the lentil mixture.

3 Cover the salad and let stand for 20 minutes to develop the flavors.

4 Mix the sliced almonds with the remaining scallions. Scatter the mixture over the salad, toss lightly, and serve, garnished with cilantro.

Nutrition per serving

Energy	364cals (1527kJ)
Carbohydrate	33g
of which sugar	1g
Fat	19g
of which saturated	2.5g
Sodium	trace
Fiber	6g

Lentils and barley with sweet potato

Warm green lentils, barley, and sweet potatoes are tossed in a pomegranate and Dijon mustard dressing, then sprinkled with bright, nutrient-packed pomegranate seeds for a delicious and filling "main dish" salad.

Serves 4–5   Prep 10 mins   Cook 40 mins

Ingredients

½ cup French green lentils

½ cup pearl barley

1 clove garlic, crushed

1 bay leaf

1 large sweet potato, peeled and diced

1 tbsp olive oil

seeds from 1 pomegranate

For the dressing

juice of 1 lemon

1 small shallot, finely chopped

1 tbsp pomegranate molasses

1 tbsp Dijon mustard

½ tsp sea salt

¼ tsp freshly ground black pepper

2 tbsp extra-virgin olive oil

Method

1 In a medium, lidded saucepan, combine the lentils, pearl barley, garlic, and bay leaf. Add water to cover by 2in (5cm). Bring to a boil, then reduce the heat to a simmer and cook for 40 minutes, or until tender. Drain, remove and discard the bay leaf, and cool slightly.

2 Meanwhile, preheat the oven to 400°F (200°C). On a baking sheet lined with parchment paper, toss the sweet potato with the oil. Roast for 30 minutes, then set aside to cool.

3 In a small bowl, whisk together the lemon juice, shallot, pomegranate molasses, mustard, salt, and black pepper. Pour in the extra-virgin olive oil, whisking continuously.

4 In a serving bowl, gently mix the lentils, barley, and sweet potatoes. Toss with three-quarters of the dressing. Sprinkle over the pomegranate seeds, drizzle with the remaining dressing, and serve warm.

Nutrition per serving

Energy 350–280cals (1407–1126kJ)	
Carbohydrate	52–42g
of which sugar	10–8g
Fat	10–8g
of which saturated	1.5–1g
Sodium	1–0.8g
Fiber	6.5–5g

On the go

Roasted sweet potato can be soft, so take care not to pack it in too tightly—otherwise, you may end up with sweet potato mash.

Pomegranate seeds

Sweet potato

Pearl barley

French green lentils

Dressing

Lentil, artichoke, and red pepper salad

The use of pantry ingredients in this salad, such as French green lentils and artichoke hearts, allows you to build a filling meal in no time. You can try a jar of already-roasted red peppers if you don't want to roast your own.

Serves 4   Prep 15 mins

Ingredients

1 × 14oz (400g) can French green lentils, drained and rinsed

1 × 14oz (400g) can artichoke hearts, drained and sliced

4 or 5 red peppers, roasted and sliced (see p15)

1–2 fresh thyme sprigs, leaves only

handful of fresh flat-leaf parsley, finely chopped

4 scallions, finely chopped

2–3 tbsp walnut oil

1 tbsp apple cider vinegar

salt and freshly ground black pepper

4–5 prosciutto slices, chopped

handful of arugula

Method

1 Put the lentils, artichoke hearts, red peppers, herbs, and scallions in a large bowl. Drizzle with the oil and vinegar, season with salt and pepper to taste, and toss gently to mix.

2 Add the prosciutto and arugula to the salad, and toss gently. Divide between 4 plates, and serve.

The oil used to preserve canned artichoke hearts also makes a delicious dressing. Try using it in place of walnut oil in this dish for an appetizing alternative.

Nutrition per serving

Energy	165cals (652kJ)
Carbohydrate	13.5g
of which sugar	3.5g
Fat	7.5g
of which saturated	1.5g
Sodium	1g
Fiber	3.5g

On the go

Prosciutto is thinly sliced and quite delicate, so it should be layered on the top of the salad, alongside the arugula.

Prosciutto and arugula

Artichokes and scallions

Red peppers

French green lentils

Walnut oil, apple cider vinegar, and herbs

Gingered fava beans with lentils

A fragrant ginger dressing lifts this pulse-based salad and, along with the inclusion of green chile, adds a gentle heat to the dish.

Serves 4   Prep 15 mins

Ingredients

½ cup frozen shelled fava beans

1 × 14oz (400g) can green or brown lentils, drained

salt and freshly ground black pepper

1 bunch of scallions, finely chopped

1 fresh green chile, seeded and finely chopped

6oz (175g) feta cheese, cut into cubes

handful of flat-leaf parsley, finely chopped

For the dressing

3 tbsp olive oil

1 tbsp white wine vinegar

1 × 1in (2.5cm) piece fresh ginger, peeled and grated

pinch of sugar (optional)

Method

1 Soak the fava beans in boiling water for 5 minutes, then drain.

2 Rinse the lentils, drain well, put into a serving bowl, and season. Add the scallions, chile, and drained fava beans, and stir well.

3 To make the dressing, put the oil, vinegar, and ginger in a small bowl. Season with salt and pepper, add a pinch of sugar (if using), and whisk until well combined. Drizzle over the salad and let stand for 10 minutes, to develop the flavors. When ready to serve, stir in the feta and parsley.

Nutrition per serving

Energy	220cals (1120kJ)
Carbohydrate	14g
of which sugar	3g
Fat	18g
of which saturated	7g
Sodium	1.1g
Fiber	5g

Flageolet beans with smoked cheese

Dainty little flageolet beans are actually unripe navy beans. They have a delicate flavor, so do not overpower them with too much smoked cheese.

Serves 4   Prep 15 mins

Ingredients

1 × 14oz (400g) can flageolet beans, drained and rinsed

1 tsp Dijon mustard

handful of flat-leaf parsley, finely chopped

salt and freshly ground black pepper

½ red onion, finely chopped

2 handfuls of watercress, rinsed, drained, and roughly chopped

1 lemon, halved

4½oz (125g) lightly smoked cheese, such as Gouda, cubed

Method

1 Put the beans in a large bowl. Add the Dijon mustard and parsley, and stir to combine. Season with salt and black pepper. Add half of the chopped onion, and stir to combine.

2 Arrange the watercress on a large serving plate or 4 individual plates. Squeeze over the juice from the lemon, and sprinkle over a pinch of salt. Spoon the bean mixture on top of the leaves, then scatter over the remaining onion. Top with the smoked cheese, and serve.

Nutrition per serving

Energy	163cals (645kJ)
Carbohydrate	9g
of which sugar	2g
Fat	8g
of which saturated	5g
Sodium	1.1g
Fiber	4.5g

Curried chickpeas with mango

This salad is perfect for anyone looking for tropical flavors and spices without the heavy sauces typical of traditional curry. The freshness provided by the mango and mint makes this fruity salad perfect for summer.

Serves 4   Prep 20 mins

Ingredients

1 × 14oz (400g) can chickpeas, drained and rinsed

1 mango, cut into cubes

1 red onion, finely chopped

handful of whole almonds, halved

handful of mint leaves, finely chopped

For the dressing

3 tbsp extra-virgin olive oil

1 tbsp apple cider vinegar

pinch of sugar

pinch of mild curry powder

salt and freshly ground black pepper

Method

1 First, make the dressing. In a small bowl, whisk together the oil and vinegar. Add the sugar and curry powder, season with salt and black pepper, and whisk until blended.

2 Put the chickpeas, mango, red onion, and almonds in a bowl, and combine. Pour over the dressing, and toss to coat. Just before serving, stir in the fresh mint leaves.

Nutrition per serving

Energy	236cals (929kJ)
Carbohydrate	18g
of which sugar	8g
Fat	14g
of which saturated	2g
Sodium	trace
Fiber	6g

On the go

Unlike other fruits, such as avocado and apple, mango does not discolor once cut, so you do not have to toss it in citrus juice before layering.

Almonds and mint

Red onion

Mango

Chickpeas

Curried dressing

Pearl barley, squash, and tomato salad

Fiber-rich pearl barley makes a great addition to warm salads like this one. The chewy grains cling to the roasted squash and tomato, adding an extra textural dimension to the meal.

Serves 2   Prep 20 mins   Cook 40 mins

Ingredients

½ small butternut squash, cut into ½in (1cm) cubes (about 10oz/300g prepared weight)

2 tbsp olive oil

salt and freshly ground black pepper

pinch of red pepper flakes

½ cup uncooked pearl barley

2 cups vegetable stock

4 plum tomatoes

3 scallions, thinly sliced

2½oz (75g) arugula

Method

1 Preheat the oven to 400°F (200°C). Place the squash in a roasting pan and drizzle 1 tablespoon of the oil over it. Season with salt and black pepper, and scatter the red pepper flakes on top. Put in the oven and cook for 30–40 minutes, until the squash is soft and browning at the edges.

2 Place the barley in a small saucepan and pour in the stock. Bring to a boil, then reduce the heat, cover, and simmer for 20–30 minutes. Add a little more stock or water, if needed.

3 Slice the tomatoes into quarters and remove the seeds. Pat the flesh dry with paper towels and place the segments in a clean roasting pan. Drizzle with the remaining oil and cook in the oven for 20–30 minutes, until soft.

4 Allow the barley to cool for 10 minutes, then stir in the squash, tomatoes, scallions, and arugula.

Nutrition per serving

Energy	345cals (1442kJ)
Carbohydrate	28g
of which sugar	14g
Fat	11g
of which saturated	2g
Sodium	0.4g
Fiber	2g

On the go

Roasted tomatoes are quite soft, and can disintegrate in a portable salad. Try throwing in some freshly chopped cherry tomatoes instead.

Arugula
Scallions
Tomatoes
Butternut squash
Pearl barley

Nutty pearl barley and lentil salad

The combination of hearty pearl barley and nutty, crunchy almonds and walnuts in this salad is well balanced by the contrasting tastes and textures of sweet, dried cranberries and salty goat cheese.

Serves 4   Prep 10 mins, plus overnight soaking and cooling   Cook 30 mins

Ingredients

⅓ cup uncooked pearl barley

1 × 14oz (400g) can green lentils, drained

¼ cup almonds, roughly chopped

¼ cup walnuts, roughly chopped

⅓ cup dried cranberries

⅓ cup soft goat cheese, crumbled

3½oz (100g) arugula leaves

Method

1 Place the barley in a bowl, cover with water, and allow to soak overnight or for at least 8 hours. Then drain, rinse under running water, and drain well again.

2 Place the barley in a lidded saucepan and cover with plenty of water. Bring to a boil, then reduce the heat to a simmer, and cover. Cook for about 30 minutes or until the barley is tender. Remove from the heat, drain any remaining water, and allow to cool completely.

3 Once cooled, place the barley and lentils in a large bowl and mix lightly to combine. Add the almonds, walnuts, and cranberries, and mix to combine. Sprinkle over the goat cheese, add the arugula, and toss lightly. Divide the salad between 4 individual plates and serve immediately.

Nutrition per serving

Energy	349cals (1420kJ)
Carbohydrate	35g
of which sugar	8.5g
Fat	15g
of which saturated	5g
Sodium	0.4g
Fiber	4.5g

Curried rice and radish salad

Thinly sliced raw vegetables not only give this rice dish plenty of crunch, but also a nutritional boost: among other benefits, uncooked cabbage is full of potassium and iron, while radishes contain B-vitamins.

Serves 4   Prep 10 mins   Cook 35 mins

Ingredients

1 cup white rice

salt and freshly ground black pepper

handful of radishes, thinly sliced

½ red cabbage, finely shredded

1 tsp medium curry powder

½ tsp cayenne pepper

3 tbsp mixed dried fruits, such as raisins and sultanas

juice of ½ lemon

¼ cup extra-virgin olive oil

handful of flat-leaf parsley, finely chopped

Method

1 Cook the rice in a pot of salted water for about 35 minutes until tender. Drain, and rinse under cold water. Drain again, and set aside to cool.

2 Put the rice in a large bowl with the radishes, cabbage, curry powder, cayenne pepper, dried fruit, lemon juice, olive oil, and parsley. Season well, stir to combine, and serve.

Nutrition per serving

Energy	206cals (829kJ)
Carbohydrate	21g
of which sugar	10g
Fat	12g
of which saturated	1.5g
Sodium	0.1g
Fiber	3g

On the go

Rinsing cooked rice washes away any excess starch left on the grains, which helps to prevent the rice sticking together once it has cooled.

Dried fruits and parsley

Red cabbage and radishes

Rice

Olive oil, lemon juice, and spices

Harissa, sorghum, and chickpea salad

Harissa spices are combined with light and chewy sorghum grains in this Middle Eastern–style salad. If sorghum is unavailable in your local supermarket, try using millet or buckwheat instead.

Serves 4   Prep 5 mins   Cook 1 hr

Ingredients

1 cup uncooked sorghum

2 red bell peppers, seeded and cut into bite-sized pieces

2 red onions, diced

1 tbsp light olive oil

2 x 14oz (400g) can chickpeas, drained

1 tbsp harissa paste

juice of 1 lemon

salt and freshly ground black pepper

3½oz (100g) arugula

¼ cup roughly chopped flat-leaf parsley, to garnish

Method

1 Rinse the sorghum under running water and place in a large, lidded saucepan. Cover with water and bring to a boil. Then reduce the heat to a simmer and cook, covered, for 50–60 minutes, until tender. Remove from the heat, drain any remaining water, and transfer to a large bowl.

2 Meanwhile, preheat the oven to 400°F (200°C). Place the red bell peppers and onions on a baking sheet. Drizzle with the oil and toss to coat. Bake in the oven for 30–40 minutes, until softened. Remove from the heat. Add the red bell peppers and onions to the sorghum and mix well.

3 Add the chickpeas and harissa paste to the sorghum mixture. Toss to combine, making sure the vegetables and chickpeas are evenly covered with the paste. Pour in the lemon juice and season to taste. Divide the arugula between 4 individual plates and top with the sorghum salad. Garnish with parsley and serve immediately.

Nutrition per serving

Energy	421cals (1612kJ)
Carbohydrate	63g
of which sugar	9.5g
Fat	8.5g
of which saturated	0.8g
Sodium	0.1g
Fiber	14g

Chickpea, red rice, and artichoke salad

This recipe features Carmargue red rice, a chewy grain with a deep maroon color and nutty flavor. As well as being a great meal in itself, the salad also makes a wonderful side for chicken dishes.

Serves 4   Prep 10 mins   Cook 35 mins

Ingredients

salt and freshly ground
  black pepper

2½ cups Carmargue red rice or
  long-grain brown rice

1 × 14oz (400g) can chickpeas,
  drained and rinsed

1 × 10oz (280g) jar roasted
  artichokes, drained

1 red chile, seeded and
  finely chopped

handful of cilantro, finely
  chopped

handful of flat-leaf parsley,
  finely chopped

2 tbsp pine nuts, toasted

½ cup feta cheese, crumbled

For the dressing

⅓ cup extra-virgin olive oil

2 tbsp white wine vinegar

juice of 1 large orange

1½ tsp coriander seeds,
  lightly crushed

1 tsp Dijon mustard

pinch of sugar

Method

1 For the dressing, place all the ingredients in a small bowl and mix well. Taste and adjust the seasoning as required.

2 Place the rice in a large pot of salted water and cook according to the package instructions until tender. Drain well and transfer to a serving bowl.

3 While the rice is still warm, stir in the chickpeas, artichokes, chile, and herbs, and mix well. Pour the dressing over the rice mixture and toss to coat. Taste and adjust the seasoning. Top with the pine nuts and feta cheese and serve.

Nutrition per serving	
Energy	710cals (2958kJ)
Carbohydrate	90g
of which sugar	7g
Fat	28g
of which saturated	5.5g
Sodium	1.3g
Fiber	5g

On the go

Before pouring the dressing into the container, reserve a little to toss with the rice so that it doesn't stick together.

Pine nuts, chile, and herbs

Artichokes and feta

Red rice

Chickpeas

Dressing

Triple-grain herbed salad bowl

This is a real good-for-you, wholesome salad mix. The combination of couscous, brown rice, and bulgur wheat creates a dish that is rich in B-vitamins, minerals, and fiber.

Serves 6   Prep 5 mins   Cook 35 mins

Ingredients

¾ cup brown rice

1 cup bulgur wheat

¾ cup couscous

4 tomatoes, diced

½ cucumber, peeled and diced

1¾oz (50g) fresh mint leaves, finely chopped

1¾oz (50g) fresh parsley, finely chopped

½ cup raisins

salt and freshly ground black pepper

Method

1 Cook the rice in a pot of salted water for about 35 minutes, until tender. Drain and rinse under cold water, then drain again and set aside to cool.

2 Meanwhile, put the bulgur wheat into a bowl and pour boiling water over it, until it is just covered. Let stand for 5 minutes while you prepare the couscous in another bowl in the same way; let this stand for 5 minutes as well. Fluff up both the grains with a fork and then mix them together with the rice.

3 Stir the tomatoes, cucumber, herbs, and raisins into the grain mixture. Taste and season, if needed.

Nutrition per serving

Energy	381cals (1385kJ)
Carbohydrate	73g
of which sugar	6g
Fat	2g
of which saturated	0.5g
Sodium	trace
Fiber	2g

On the go

You can include the grains as three separate layers if you prefer, but by mixing them together, you guarantee a varied blend of textures.

Herbs

Cucumber

Tomato and raisins

Three-grain mixture

Kale and freekeh salad *with garlic tahini*

Chopped salads are easy to throw together and a great way to use up surplus ingredients in the fridge. Beautifully summery, this salad is best served when zucchini and sweet corn are in their peak season.

Serves 4   Prep 20 mins, plus cooling   Cook 30 mins

Ingredients

1 cup uncooked freekeh

2½ cups vegetable stock

1½ cups fresh sweet corn

salt and freshly ground black pepper

1 tbsp olive oil

¾ cup almonds, chopped

10–12 kale leaves chopped

1 × 14oz (400g) can chickpeas, chopped

4–6 scallions, chopped

2 zucchini, diced

For the dressing

3 tbsp tahini

1 garlic clove, pressed

2 tbsp lemon juice

1 tsp soy sauce

1 tsp toasted sesame oil

Nutrition per serving

Energy	576cals (2270kJ)
Carbohydrate	44g
of which sugar	6g
Fat	30g
of which saturated	3.5g
Sodium	1g
Fiber	14g

Method

1 Rinse the freekeh under cold running water, drain well, and place in a lidded saucepan. Add the stock and bring to a boil. Reduce the heat to a simmer, cover, and cook for about 20 minutes. Remove from the heat and set aside for 5 minutes, then uncover and allow to cool.

2 Cook the sweet corn in a large saucepan of boiling salted water for 10 minutes or until tender. Remove from the pan and rinse under cold running water.

3 Place the dressing ingredients in a small bowl, add 2 tablespoons of water, and whisk until well combined. Taste, season as necessary, and set aside.

4 Heat the olive oil in a small nonstick frying pan over low heat. Add the almonds and toast for 2–3 minutes, or until the nuts are lightly browned. Remove from the heat and allow to cool.

5 Place the kale in a large bowl and drizzle with some of the dressing. Toss well to coat. Then add the sweet corn, almonds, chickpeas, scallions, and zucchini. Drizzle with more of the dressing and toss well to coat. Add the freekeh and the remaining dressing and toss well to coat. Serve immediately.

Fruit and vegetables

Salad staples like leafy greens and tomatoes sit
alongside peaches, beets, and butternut squash
in this selection of recipes packed with a rainbow
of fruits and vegetables. Try a few of these, and you
will reach your five-a-day target in no time.

Swiss chard and sweet potato bowl

As the nights draw in and the temperature drops, enjoy this nutritious and perfect fall-weather salad bowl, featuring fiber-rich Swiss chard, which is high in vitamin K and antioxidant carotenoids.

Serves 4   Prep 5–10 mins   Cook 25 mins

Ingredients

1 tbsp olive oil, plus extra to drizzle

2 shallots, peeled and finely chopped

1 tsp coriander seeds, crushed

1 chile, seeded and finely chopped

2 garlic cloves, crushed

2 large sweet potatoes, peeled and cut into cubes

9oz (250g) Swiss chard, stalks removed and finely chopped, and leaves thinly sliced

salt and freshly ground black pepper

Method

1 Heat the olive oil with 1 tablespoon of water over low heat in a medium saucepan with a lid. Add the shallots and coriander seeds and cook, stirring occasionally, until the shallots soften.

2 Add the chile and garlic, and cook for 1 minute. Add the sweet potatoes and cook over medium heat for about 5 minutes, adding a dash of water if necessary. Then add the chopped chard stalks, cover, and cook for 10 minutes.

3 When the sweet potatoes are almost cooked, add the shredded chard leaves, cover, and let wilt for about 3 minutes. Remove from the heat, season well, drizzle with a few drops of olive oil, and serve.

Nutrition per serving

Energy	194cals (823kJ)
Carbohydrate	33g
of which sugar	9g
Fat	6g
of which saturated	1g
Sodium	0.5g
Fiber	5g

Eggplant salad

By steaming eggplants instead of roasting or frying them in oil, they remain incredibly tender—and far healthier, too. For a Greek-style salad bowl, try replacing the goat cheese and sesame seeds with feta cheese and pine nuts.

Serves 6   Prep 15 mins   Cook 10 mins

Ingredients

2 medium eggplants, peeled and cut into ¾in (2cm) cubes

½ cup soft goat cheese, crumbled

2 ripe tomatoes, seeded and diced

1 small red onion, finely diced

handful of flat-leaf parsley, finely chopped

½ cup walnuts, lightly toasted and chopped

1 tbsp sesame seeds, lightly toasted

salt and freshly ground black pepper

For the dressing

1 garlic clove, crushed

salt and freshly ground black pepper

¼ cup walnut oil

juice of 1 lemon

Method

1 Cook the eggplant in a covered steamer basket placed over simmering water for 10 minutes. Let cool slightly and then gently squeeze the cubes to remove as much water as possible.

2 Combine all the salad ingredients in a mixing bowl and toss gently. Whisk together the dressing ingredients and toss with the salad. Season to taste with salt and pepper.

Nutrition per serving

Energy	218cals (863kJ)
Carbohydrate	4.9g
of which sugar	4.5g
Fat	19g
of which saturated	3.6g
Sodium	0.2g
Fiber	4g

On the go

The eggplant cubes should be completely cool before packing. Place them on a layer of paper towels to soak up excess water.

Sesame seeds and parsley

Goat cheese and walnuts

Tomatoes and onion

Eggplants

Dressing

Red pepper salad

In this Spanish dish, sweet red bell peppers are gently stewed, and then served cold. It is wonderful as tapas, or as a side dish with a piece of grilled steak or meaty fish, such as tuna.

Serves 4   Prep 10 mins   Cook 25 mins

Ingredients

3 tbsp extra-virgin olive oil

6 red bell peppers, seeded and cut into large strips

2 garlic cloves, finely chopped

9oz (250g) ripe tomatoes, peeled, seeded, and chopped

2 tbsp chopped parsley

salt and freshly ground black pepper

1 tbsp sherry vinegar

Method

1 Heat the oil in a large frying pan, add the peppers and garlic, and fry over low heat for 5 minutes, stirring, then add the tomatoes. Increase the heat, bring to a simmer, then reduce the heat to low, cover, and cook for 12–15 minutes.

2 Stir in the parsley, season well with salt and pepper, and cook for 2 more minutes. Using a slotted spoon, remove the peppers, and arrange in a serving dish.

3 Add the vinegar to the pan, increase the heat, and simmer the sauce for 5–7 minutes, or until it has reduced and thickened. Pour the sauce over the peppers and allow to cool before serving.

Nutrition per serving

Energy	143cals (547kJ)
Carbohydrate	11g
of which sugar	11g
Fat	9g
of which saturated	1g
Sodium	trace
Fiber	5.5g

Grilled vegetable and spinach bowl

When cooking barbecue, you don't need to create endless variations of "meat on bread." This salad bucks the trend with a rich, filling, and hearty dish that can be enjoyed by vegetarians and meat-eaters alike.

Serves 4   *Prep 30 mins*   *Cook 15 mins*

Ingredients

2 large eggplants, cut into slices ½in (1mm) thick

salt and freshly ground black pepper

4 mixed bell peppers, halved and seeded

½ cup olive oil

2 sprigs of fresh oregano

1 zucchini, about 10oz (300g), cut into diagonal slices ¼in (5mm) thick

6 fresh asparagus spears, trimmed and boiled

4 canned artichoke hearts, cut into wedges

4 handfuls of baby spinach leaves

12 black olives

1 small red onion, sliced into thin rounds

For the dressing

3 tbsp olive oil

1 tbsp freshly squeezed lemon juice

1 tbsp chopped fresh dill

2 scallions, thinly sliced

Method

1 Preheat the grill. Place the eggplant slices in a colander, sprinkle over salt, and set aside for 15 minutes. Rinse and pat dry with paper towels. Meanwhile, toss the peppers in 4 tablespoons of oil, the oregano, and salt and pepper.

2 Grill the peppers for 10 minutes. Allow to cool, then peel and slice into strips. Set aside. Brush the eggplant and zucchini slices with oil, and grill for 2–3 minutes on each side, until starting to char. Set aside. Lower the temperature and brush the grill with a little oil. Add the asparagus and cook for 5 minutes, turning them as they char. Finally, add the artichokes, and cook for 2–3 minutes on each side.

3 Combine the grilled vegetables with the spinach, olives, and onion in a serving bowl. Whisk together the dressing ingredients, pour over the salad, and toss gently to coat.

Nutrition per serving	
Energy	474cals (1851kJ)
Carbohydrate	17g
of which sugar	16g
Fat	39g
of which saturated	6g
Sodium	0.4g
Fiber	13g

On the go

This is an unusual portable salad, perfect for enjoying barbecue leftovers. Make sure everything is cold and dry before layering.

- Spinach
- Artichokes and olives
- Eggplants and zucchinis
- Asparagus and bell peppers
- Dressing

Celery root and mustard remoulade

Also known as celeriac, celery root has an earthy crunch that works well in remoulade: a quick, healthy, and delicious no-cook salad. Serve it over crisp lettuce or watercress, or spread on toast.

Serves 10   Prep 10 mins

Ingredients

⅓ cup mayonnaise

2 tbsp extra-virgin olive oil

2 tbsp Dijon mustard

juice of 1 lemon

2 tbsp finely chopped
   cornichon pickles

1 tbsp finely grated onion

1 tbsp finely chopped
   flat-leaf parsley

salt and freshly ground
   black pepper

1 celery root, about 1½lb (675g)

lettuce leaves, to serve

Method

1 In a large bowl, whisk together the mayonnaise, extra-virgin olive oil, Dijon mustard, lemon juice, cornichon pickles, grated onion, flat-leaf parsley, and salt, and black pepper. Set the remoulade sauce aside.

2 Wash and peel the celery root, then quarter it. Working quickly, grate each quarter into the bowl with the sauce. Toss and serve over lettuce leaves immediately. Once made, this dish will keep in the fridge for up to 2 days.

Nutrition per serving

Energy	95cals (363kJ)
Carbohydrate	2g
of which sugar	2g
Fat	8g
of which saturated	0.8g
Sodium	0.6g
Fiber	3.5g

Roasted beet and orange salad

Sweet beets combine with bright orange segments and toasted walnuts for a delicious and sophisticated salad that is packed with superfoods.

Serves 4   Prep 10 mins   Cook 30 mins

Ingredients

4 large beets
1 tbsp olive oil
1 cup walnut halves
2 seedless navel oranges
1 shallot, finely minced
juice of 1 lemon
1 tsp Dijon mustard
1 tsp sea salt
½ tsp freshly ground
    black pepper
¼ cup extra-virgin olive oil
7oz (200g) baby salad leaves
    or torn lettuce

Nutrition per serving

Energy	404cals (1607kJ)
Carbohydrate	19g
of which sugar	18g
Fat	31g
of which saturated	4g
Sodium	1.6g
Fiber	7g

Method

1 Preheat the oven to 400°F (200°C). Scrub the beets but do not peel. Place in a baking dish, drizzle with the olive oil, and roast for 30–40 minutes or until easily pierced with a fork. Remove from the oven and set aside.

2 Reduce the oven temperature to 350°F (180°C). Spread the walnuts in a single layer on a baking sheet, and toast for 7 minutes or until golden, turning the nuts once. Allow to cool slightly, and chop coarsely.

3 Zest one orange and set aside. On a chopping board, carefully segment both oranges (see p12), stopping occasionally to pour juice from the board into a bowl. Set aside the orange segments.

4 In the bowl with the reserved orange juice, whisk together the orange zest, shallot, lemon juice, Dijon mustard, salt, and black pepper. Slowly drizzle in the remaining olive oil, whisking constantly.

5 Peel the beets, cut into ½in (1cm) wedges, and toss with the orange segments and half of the vinaigrette.

6 Arrange the lettuce on 4 individual plates, drizzle with the remaining dressing, and divide the beet mixture evenly over the leaves. Sprinkle each salad with one-quarter of the walnuts, and serve immediately.

Grilled broccoli rabe *with romesco*

A tasty vegetarian recipe, this salad can be served as a filling main meal or even an impressive side. The flavor of the broccoli is enhanced by grilling and is well paired with the spicy Spanish dressing and fluffy barley.

Serves 6   Prep 10 mins, plus soaking   Cook 1 hr 5 mins

Ingredients

1 cup uncooked barley

salt and freshly ground
 black pepper

1lb 5oz (600g) broccoli rabe

2 tbsp extra-virgin olive oil

juice of ½ lemon

For the dressing

1½ dried ancho chiles, seeded

½ cup almonds, sliced

3½oz (100g) roasted red
 peppers from a jar

1 × 14oz (400g) can chopped
 tomatoes

2 tbsp sherry vinegar

2 tbsp extra-virgin olive oil

pinch of smoked paprika

Nutrition per serving

Energy	301cals (1204kJ)
Carbohydrate	33g
of which sugar	5g
Fat	13g
of which saturated	2g
Sodium	trace
Fiber	4.5g

Method

1 Place the barley in a large pot and cover with 3 cups of salted water. Bring to a boil, then reduce the heat to a simmer, cover, and cook for about 50 minutes or until almost all the water has been absorbed. Remove from the heat. Cover and set aside.

2 Meanwhile, for the dressing, place the chiles in a small bowl, and cover with water. Let soak for 10 minutes, then drain and discard the water. Dice the chiles and set them aside. In a nonstick frying pan, toast the almonds over medium-low heat for 3–4 minutes. Transfer to a food processor and pulse until they form a coarse flour.

3 Add the chiles, peppers, tomatoes, vinegar, oil, and paprika to the food processor. Season with salt and pepper. Pulse until the mixture is smooth, but retains a little texture. Transfer the dressing to a bowl and set aside.

4 Place the broccoli in a large bowl. Drizzle with the oil, season to taste, and toss to coat. Heat a griddle pan over medium–high heat. Grill the broccoli for 3–5 minutes on each side, until tender and starting to brown.

5 Remove the broccoli from the heat and drizzle with the lemon juice. On a large serving dish, spread out the barley and top with the broccoli. Pour over the desired amount of romesco dressing. Serve immediately with the remaining dressing on the side.

Mediterranean salad boats

The flavors of the Mediterranean come together in this quick and easy salad that is as colorful as it is satisfying. Its unusual presentation, inside romaine-leaf "boats", also makes it a fun veggie-packed dish to serve to children.

Serves 4   Prep 15 mins

Ingredients

1 large tomato, seeded and diced

1 cucumber, diced

1 red bell pepper, seeded and diced

2¼oz (70g) Kalamata olives, pitted and halved

¾ cup feta cheese, crumbled

1 cup prepared quinoa

2 tbsp extra-virgin olive oil

2 tbsp lemon juice

1 garlic clove, crushed

1 tbsp chopped oregano

salt and freshly ground black pepper

1 romaine heart, leaves separated

Method

1 Place the tomatoes, cucumber, red pepper, olives, feta, and quinoa in a large bowl and toss to combine. Place the oil, lemon juice, garlic, and oregano in a separate bowl and whisk to combine.

2 Pour the oil mixture over the salad and toss to coat. Season to taste. Divide the salad between 4 individual plates. Top the romaine leaves with equal amounts of the mixture and serve immediately.

Nutrition per serving

Energy	279cals (1207kJ)
Carbohydrate	19g
of which sugar	4g
Fat	19g
of which saturated	6g
Sodium	1.2g
Fiber	3g

Neapolitan Christmas salad

This festive salad is known as "insalata di rinfozo" in Italian. It is traditionally made on Christmas Eve and replenished throughout the following days, but can be enjoyed at any time of year as a wholesome vegetarian dish.

Serves 6   Prep 10 mins   Cook 20 mins

Ingredients

- 1 head cauliflower, broken into small florets
- 1 garlic clove, finely chopped, plus more to taste
- ½ small red onion, sliced paper thin
- 4 roasted red peppers, thinly sliced
- 1 cup pitted black olives
- 1 cup pitted green Cerignola olives
- ¼ cup salted capers, rinsed and drained
- ½ cup extra-virgin olive oil
- ¼ cup red wine vinegar, or to taste
- ¼ cup finely chopped flat-leaf parsley
- ½ tsp freshly ground black pepper, plus more to taste

Method

1 In a pot with a tight-fitting lid, bring 1in (2.5cm) of water to a boil over a medium-high heat. Place the cauliflower in a steamer basket, place in the pot, and steam for about 6 minutes or until tender. Transfer the cauliflower to a large bowl, and immediately toss with the garlic and red onion.

2 Using a silicone spatula, gently stir in the roasted red peppers, both types of olives, and capers. Drizzle with the extra-virgin olive oil, and toss gently.

3 Add the vinegar, flat-leaf parsley, and black pepper, and toss again. Taste and add more vinegar or black pepper, if desired. Serve immediately, or refrigerate for up to 1 week.

Nutrition per serving

Energy	278cals (1118kJ)
Carbohydrate	10g
of which sugar	7g
Fat	24g
of which saturated	3.5g
Sodium	2g
Fiber	4.5g

On the go

Pack this salad for your first day back in the office after the holidays, so you can carry on the festivities a little longer.

- Capers
- Onion and garlic
- Olives and peppers
- Cauliflower
- Oil, vinegar, and herbs

Grated carrot and beet salad

Richly colored and packed with beneficial antioxidants, this salad is a unique alternative to coleslaw. Try to source young, fresh produce if possible to maximize the taste and crunch of the raw grated vegetables.

Serves 4   Prep 30 mins   Cook 3–4 mins

Ingredients

1lb 5oz (600g) carrots, trimmed and scrubbed

1lb 5oz (600g) beets, peeled and halved

small bunch of flat-leaf parsley, chopped

For the dressing

⅓ cup extra-virgin olive oil, plus 1 tsp for toasting the seeds

3 tbsp balsamic vinegar

1 garlic clove, crushed (optional)

¼ cup sunflower or pumpkin seeds

1 tsp soy sauce (optional)

salt and freshly ground black pepper

Method

1 Coarsely grate the raw vegetables and combine in a large bowl.

2 For the dressing, put the ⅓ cup of oil, vinegar, and garlic (if using) in a screw-top jar, put the lid on tightly, and shake.

3 Gently heat the remaining olive oil in a small frying pan and toast the seeds for 3–4 minutes over medium heat, stirring frequently to prevent burning. Add the soy sauce at the end of cooking (if using). Most of the soy sauce will evaporate, leaving a salty taste and extra browning for the seeds.

4 Add the parsley to the carrots and beets. Shake the vinaigrette again, pour over the vegetables, then season to taste. Toss the salad gently, scatter the toasted seeds over the top, and serve.

Nutrition per serving

Energy	370cals (1453kJ)
Carbohydrate	27g
of which sugar	23g
Fat	24g
of which saturated	3.5g
Sodium	0.5g
Fiber	11g

On the go

Store this salad in your office kitchen fridge, but allow it to come back up to room temperature before eating.

Seeds

Carrot and beet mixture

Dressing

Shaved fennel
with balsamic marinade

This fresh salad makes a fantastic side dish for grilled fish. Alternatively, the addition of crumbled goat cheese and a few slices of apple or pear can turn it into a light lunch in itself.

Serves 6   Prep 10 mins, plus marinating

Ingredients

1 fennel bulb, peeled and thinly sliced

½ tbsp aged balsamic vinegar

3 tbsp extra-virgin olive oil

1 garlic clove, crushed

sea salt and freshly ground black pepper

5½oz (150g) mixed salad leaves, such as watercress, baby spinach, arugula, or mâche (lamb's lettuce)

goat cheese (optional)

apple or pear slices (optional)

Method

1 In a bowl, toss the fennel with a few drops of balsamic vinegar, 1 tablespoon of oil, and the garlic, then season with salt and pepper. Set aside to marinate for at least 1 hour before serving.

2 To serve, mix the salad leaves, marinated fennel, and the remaining oil and vinegar, then season to taste with salt and pepper. Divide between 6 individual serving plates. Scatter over goat cheese and fruit slices, if desired.

Nutrition per serving

Energy	60cals (238kJ)
Carbohydrate	1g
of which sugar	1g
Fat	5.5g
of which saturated	1g
Sodium	trace
Fiber	1.5g

On the go

If you want to include apple or pear slices in your salad, remember to toss in a little citrus juice beforehand.

Salad leaves

Goat cheese (optional)

Fruit slices (optional)

Marinated fennel

Shredded carrot and cabbage *with nuts*

This no-cook salad packs plenty of crunch, as well as plenty of health benefits. Cabbage provides vitamins B6, C, and K, while carrots are packed with beta-carotene—and by serving them raw, you maximize the nutritional boost.

Serves 4   Prep 15 mins

Ingredients

2 sweet apples

4 carrots, peeled and grated

1 small white cabbage, shredded

handful of sunflower seeds

handful of salted or
  dry-roasted peanuts

For the dressing

1 tbsp light soy sauce

1 tbsp Thai fish sauce

1 fresh green chile, seeded
  and finely chopped

1 garlic clove, grated or
  finely chopped

juice of 2 limes

1–2 tsp sugar

handful of cilantro, finely
  chopped

salt and freshly ground
  black pepper

Method

1 First, make the dressing. Put all the dressing ingredients in a small bowl, and mix thoroughly until the sugar has dissolved. Taste and season with salt and black pepper as needed. If it needs sweetening, add more sugar; if it needs saltiness, add a little more fish sauce.

2 Quarter and core the apples, then chop into bite-sized pieces. Put in a bowl with the carrots, cabbage, and sunflower seeds. Toss well. Drizzle with the dressing, and toss to coat. Transfer to a serving dish, and scatter the peanuts over the top.

Nutrition per serving	
Energy	215cals (815kJ)
Carbohydrate	27g
of which sugar	25g
Fat	7g
of which saturated	1g
Sodium	1.7g
Fiber	10g

On the go

You can combine these salad ingredients for a simple all-in-one lunch, or layer them in a jar or tall container if you prefer.

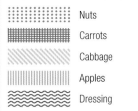

Nuts

Carrots

Cabbage

Apples

Dressing

Artichoke salad with lemon juice

Freshly grown artichokes are a summer treat. For the rest of the year, you can always use prepared artichokes preserved in jars instead, and substitute the olive oil in the recipe for the preserving oil for added flavor.

Serves 4   Prep 25 mins, plus cooling   Cook 10 mins

Ingredients

4 artichokes

3 lemons

sea salt

2 large handfuls of arugula

scant 1oz (25g) Parmesan cheese

2 tbsp extra-virgin olive oil

1 tbsp balsamic vinegar

freshly ground black pepper

Method

1 Trim the artichoke stalks and hard outside leaves (about 5–6 layers), until you reach the paler, more tender ones. Cut about 1in (2.5cm) off the spiny tips and discard. Then slice in half and using a teaspoon, carefully remove the choke and discard. Place the artichoke hearts in a bowl and pour the juice of 2 lemons over them.

2 Bring a pot of water to a boil. Add 1 tsp salt and the juice of the remaining lemon. Place the artichokes into the pan and cook for 10 minutes, or until tender. Drain well and set aside to cool.

3 When the artichokes are cool enough to handle, carefully cut them into quarters.

4 Divide the arugula and artichokes between 4 individual plates. Using a vegetable peeler, shave pieces of Parmesan over each salad. Drizzle with olive oil and balsamic vinegar, and season to taste with salt and pepper.

Nutrition per serving

Energy	151cals (597kJ)
Carbohydrate	2g
of which sugar	2g
Fat	13g
of which saturated	3g
Sodium	1g
Fiber	4g

Fennel and peach salad

This pretty fennel and peach salad from the French Riviera makes a refreshing appetizer on a hot summer's day. For a meat-free version of this recipe, replace the ham with shavings of Parmesan cheese.

Serves 4   Prep 15–20 mins

Ingredients

2 small fennel bulbs, trimmed at the bottom and very thinly sliced

juice and finely grated zest of ½ lemon

1 tbsp extra-virgin olive oil

salt and freshly ground black pepper

2 ripe peaches or nectarines, halved, cored, and sliced

1 tbsp chopped flat-leaf parsley

½ tbsp chopped mint leaves

1 slice of cured ham about ¼in/5mm thick, such as prosciutto crudo, Serrano, or smoked ham, diced

Method

1 In a shallow bowl, toss the fennel with the lemon juice and zest, oil, and a little salt. Add the peaches or nectarines, sprinkle over half the herbs, and season with pepper. Toss lightly.

2 Arrange on a serving plate. Scatter the ham and the remaining herbs over top. Serve immediately.

Nutrition per serving

Energy	78cals/326kJ
Carbohydrate	7g
of which sugar	6.5g
Fat	3.5g
of which saturated	0.5g
Sodium	0.3g
Fiber	4g

Tomato and farfalle pasta salad

This is a simple, fresh salad that can be whipped up in minutes if you have leftover pasta on hand. It is perfect for children, and is endlessly adaptable—try adding peppers, red onion, or cooked zucchini.

Serves 4   Prep 10 mins   Cook 10 mins

Ingredients

9oz (250g) farfalle pasta

5 tomatoes, peeled (p15)

handful of fresh flat-leaf parsley, finely chopped

handful of fresh basil leaves, torn

2 garlic cloves, grated

salt and freshly ground black pepper

extra-virgin olive oil, to taste

Method

1 Cook the pasta in a pot of boiling salted water for 10 minutes, or until al dente. Drain, and return to the pot.

2 Coarsely chop the tomatoes and add to the pasta along with the parsley, basil leaves, and garlic. Season with salt and black pepper, and toss with some olive oil to coat before serving.

Nutrition per serving

Energy	296cals (1193kJ)
Carbohydrate	49g
of which sugar	5g
Fat	6.5g
of which saturated	1g
Sodium	trace
Fiber	4g

On the go

Before removing the container lid, lightly shake the salad to distribute the olive oil through the pasta and tomatoes.

Tomatoes

Pasta

Olive oil, garlic, and herbs

Shiitake mushrooms with wilted spinach

Baby spinach is quickly wilted in a flavorful dressing of shiitake mushrooms accented with walnuts, Dijon mustard, and tangy apple cider vinegar. Add some cooked quinoa for a hearty dinner.

Serves 3   Prep 5 mins   Cook 10 mins

Ingredients

1 tbsp sesame oil

1 × 4oz (115g) pkg. shiitake mushrooms, stems removed and thinly sliced

1 cup walnuts, finely chopped

1 clove garlic, finely chopped

1 small red onion, halved and thinly sliced

salt and freshly ground black pepper

1 tbsp whole-grain Dijon mustard

¼ cup apple cider vinegar

½ cup extra-virgin olive oil

12oz (360g) baby spinach, washed and drained

cooked quinoa, to serve (optional)

Method

1 Heat the sesame oil in a medium frying pan over a medium-high heat. Add the shiitake mushrooms and stir for 2 minutes.

2 Add the walnuts and garlic to the pan, and stir for 2 minutes. Adjust the heat as needed.

3 Add the onion, salt, mustard, and apple cider vinegar, and bring to a boil. Remove from the heat.

4 Slowly stir in the extra-virgin olive oil. Add the baby spinach, toss with hot mushroom mixture until wilted, and season with black pepper. Serve with quinoa, if you wish.

Nutrition per serving

Energy	633cals (2512kJ)
Carbohydrate	6g
of which sugar	5g
Fat	60g
of which saturated	7.5g
Sodium	1g
Fiber	11g

Panzanella *with red wine vinaigrette*

Good-quality bread is a joy, and even when it is a bit stale, it can be used in this delectable Italian salad. The vinaigrette moistens and refreshes the bread, making it the perfect partner for fresh, juicy tomatoes.

Serves 4–6   *Prep 15 mins, plus standing*

Ingredients

12oz (350g) unsliced stale dense-textured bread, such as ciabatta or sourdough, roughly torn into bite-sized pieces

1lb 5oz (600g) mixed tomatoes, roughly chopped into bite-sized chunks

1 red onion, finely chopped

2 garlic cloves, finely chopped

2 tbsp capers in brine, drained

salt and freshly ground black pepper

1 bunch of basil, roughly torn

For the dressing

⅓ cup extra-virgin olive oil

3 tbsp red wine vinegar

½ tsp mustard powder

½ tsp sugar

Method

1 Place the bread, tomatoes, onion, garlic, and capers in a large serving bowl. Season well and stir to combine.

2 Place the dressing ingredients in a small bowl, season, and stir well. Pour over the bread and tomato mixture and stir to coat.

3 Set aside for at least 10 minutes, or up to 2 hours, at room temperature, to allow the flavors to mingle. Stir the basil leaves into the salad just before serving.

Nutrition per serving	
Energy	396cals (1664kJ)
Carbohydrate	47g
of which sugar	8.5g
Fat	19g
of which saturated	3g
Sodium	1.7g
Fiber	4.5g

On the go

The bread will absorb the vinaigrette while it sits. Give the container a light shake before lunch to coat the other ingredients.

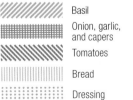

Basil

Onion, garlic, and capers

Tomatoes

Bread

Dressing

Chili-crumbed spinach salad

This simple spinach and tomato salad is elevated to another dimension with the addition of toasted chili breadcrumbs and pine nuts. It is the perfect accompaniment for lamb, or simply add some cheese for a vegetarian lunch.

Serves 4   Prep 15 mins   Cook 10 mins

Ingredients

2–3 slices of bread, torn

pinch of red chili pepper flakes

salt and freshly ground
  black pepper

9oz (250g) baby spinach leaves

handful of juicy raisins
  (optional)

3½oz (100g) sun-dried
  tomatoes, roughly chopped

⅓ cup pine nuts, toasted

For the dressing

3 tbsp extra-virgin olive oil

1 tbsp orange juice

pinch of sugar

Method

1 Mix the dressing ingredients together in a bowl, taste, and season as needed. Set aside. Preheat the oven to 400°F (200°C).

2 To make the breadcrumb topping, put the bread in a food processor and pulse to form crumbs. Pour the crumbs into a roasting pan and bake for 5–10 minutes or until golden. Don't let them brown. Stir the red pepper flakes and salt and pepper into the crumbs. Set aside.

3 To assemble the salad, pour the dressing into a large salad bowl and swirl it around. Add the spinach leaves and shake to coat. Add the raisins (if using) and sun-dried tomatoes, and toss gently. Top with the pine nuts, sprinkle over breadcrumbs, and serve.

For a more substantial salad, add some cheese: Parmesan shavings, crumbled feta, or torn buffalo mozzarella all work well.

Nutrition per serving

Energy	270cals (1124kJ)
Carbohydrate	17.5g
of which sugar	9.5g
Fat	19g
of which saturated	2g
Sodium	0.8g
Fiber	4g

Fattoush

The lemony taste of sumac is hard to beat. The spice is an essential component of this traditional Middle Eastern dish, along with sweet pomegranate syrup and crisp toasted flatbread.

Serves 6   Prep 15 mins

Ingredients

handful of fresh lettuce leaves

2–3 tomatoes, skinned and sliced

1 red or green bell pepper, seeded and chopped

4–5 scallions, trimmed and sliced

small bunch of flat-leaf parsley, coarsely chopped

2 thin flatbreads, such as pita breads

2–3 tbsp olive oil

juice of 1 lemon

1–2 garlic cloves, crushed

1 tsp cumin seeds, crushed

salt and freshly ground black pepper

1–2 tbsp pomegranate syrup

2 tsp sumac

Method

1 Arrange the lettuce leaves, tomatoes, peppers, and scallions in a wide, shallow bowl and sprinkle over the parsley. Lightly toast the flatbreads, break them into bite-sized pieces, and scatter them over the salad.

2 In a small bowl, combine the oil and lemon juice with the garlic and cumin seeds. Season well and pour over the salad. Drizzle the salad with the pomegranate syrup and sprinkle over the sumac. Toss the salad gently just before serving.

Nutrition per serving

Energy	120cals (502kJ)
Carbohydrate	17g
of which sugar	5g
Fat	4g
of which saturated	0.6g
Sodium	0.2g
Fiber	2g

On the go

Store the flatbread pieces in a separate container to keep them crisp until you are ready to eat.

- Flatbread pieces
- Lettuce, parsley, and spices
- Bell pepper, scallions, and tomatoes
- Oil and lemon juice
- Pomegranate syrup

Waldorf salad

Created at the Waldorf Astoria Hotel in New York, this creamy and crunchy salad has been a favorite for over 100 years. It goes well with grilled chicken if you need something a bit more filling.

Serves 4   *Prep 15 mins*

Ingredients

2 large apples

4 celery sticks, thinly sliced

25 red seedless grapes, halved

2 tbsp toasted and crushed walnuts

¼ cup mayonnaise

juice of 1 lemon, plus extra for serving

salt and freshly ground black pepper

2 hearts romaine lettuce

Method

1 Remove the cores of the apples using a corer. Then, using a sharp knife, cut the apples into slices of an even thickness. Stack the slices, a few at a time, and cut lengthwise through the pile and then crosswise, making equal-sized cubes.

2 Put the apples, celery, grapes, and walnuts in a bowl. Add the mayonnaise and lemon juice and toss well to combine. Season with salt and pepper to taste.

3 Roughly chop the lettuce and divide between 4 individual plates. Serve the fruit and nut mixture on each bed of lettuce with a squeeze of lemon.

Nutrition per serving

Energy	220cals (890kJ)
Carbohydrate	13.5g
of which sugar	13.5g
Fat	17g
of which saturated	1.5g
Sodium	0.1g
Fiber	2.5g

On the go

Coat the apples with the lemon-mayo mixture at the bottom of the container so they do not get discolored.

Lettuce

Walnuts

Celery and grapes

Apples

Lemon-mayonnaise mixture

Shepherd's salad

Also called Arabic salad, this dish is popular in Turkey and the Middle East. Laden with fresh herbs and spices, it's a perfect complement to some grilled or barbecued lamb, or lemony chicken.

Serves 4   Prep 20 mins

Ingredients

1 large cucumber, peeled

15 baby cherry tomatoes

1 head sweet romaine lettuce

12 black olives, pitted
   and chopped

3 scallions, chopped

2 tbsp finely chopped flat-leaf
   parsley

2 tbsp finely chopped cilantro

2 tbsp finely chopped mint

2 tbsp chopped purslane
   or arugula

For the dressing

½ garlic clove, crushed

½ tsp sweet paprika

½ tsp ground sumac

½ tsp sugar

½ tsp ground cumin

2 tbsp lemon juice and
   1 tsp grated lemon zest

½ cup extra-virgin olive oil

sea salt and freshly ground
   black pepper

Method

1 In a bowl, mix together all the ingredients for the dressing, and season with salt and pepper to taste. Leave the mixture to rest while you prepare the salad ingredients.

2 Quarter the cucumber lengthwise, then scoop out and discard the seeds. Cut the flesh into small, neat chunks. Reserve on a plate. Halve the tomatoes, scoop out and discard some of the seeds, and add to the cucumber. Tear or chop the lettuce into bite-sized pieces.

3 Stir the dressing. Put a layer of lettuce in the bowl (do not toss), then scatter in some olives and scallions. Sprinkle over some parsley, cilantro, mint, and purslane or arugula. Add half the cucumber and tomatoes. Continue adding the ingredients until everything is in the bowl. Toss the salad just before serving.

Nutrition per serving

Energy	227cals (921kJ)
Carbohydrate	4g
of which sugar	3.5g
Fat	22g
of which saturated	3g
Sodium	0.2g
Fiber	2g

Orange salad with olives

Refreshing orange salads are popular in the southern Mediterranean. They are often served alongside stews and grilled meat or fish, but can easily be enjoyed as a fruity, light lunch, if you prefer.

Serves 4   Prep 15–20 mins, plus standing

Ingredients

1 small–medium red onion, thinly sliced

2 ripe oranges

8–10 green olives

juice and finely grated zest of ½ lemon

2 tbsp extra-virgin olive oil

salt and freshly ground black pepper

handful of flat-leaf parsley, chopped, to serve

Method

1 Place the onion in a bowl of cold water. Using a sharp knife, remove the peel and pith from the oranges, and slice thinly.

2 Place the oranges in a shallow serving dish. Drain the onion slices, place on a double layer of paper towels, and pat dry. Arrange the slices on the oranges. Scatter the olives on top.

3 In a small cup, combine the lemon juice and zest and the olive oil. Season to taste and drizzle over the salad. If you like, scatter with the chopped parsley. Let stand for 5 minutes before serving.

Nutrition per serving

Energy	97cals (406kJ)
Carbohydrate	8g
of which sugar	7g
Fat	6.5g
of which saturated	1g
Sodium	2g
Fiber	1.6g

Spinach with pine nuts and raisins

This simple salad is a traditional Italian Jewish side dish, popular for its contrasting textures—from plump, juicy raisins to crunchy nuts.

Serves 4   Prep 5 mins   Cook 10 mins

Ingredients

1 tbsp olive oil

3 tbsp raisins

3 tbsp pine nuts

3 tbsp dry sherry

7oz (200g) fresh spinach, rinsed and roughly chopped

1 tsp paprika

salt and freshly ground black pepper

Method

1 Combine the oil, raisins, and pine nuts in a shallow frying pan over medium heat. When the raisins and pine nuts start to sizzle, cook for 2 minutes, stirring constantly. Carefully add the sherry and cook until the liquid has reduced by half.

2 Add the spinach and paprika and cook, stirring constantly, for 5 minutes, or until the spinach has wilted. Season with salt and black pepper and serve hot or cold.

If you don't have sherry, use some dessert wine, white wine, or a splash of white wine vinegar to add sharpness.

Nutrition per serving

Energy	161cals (640kJ)
Carbohydrate	8g
of which sugar	8g
Fat	11g
of which saturated	1g
Sodium	0.1g
Fiber	1.5g

Endive salad with spinach and pears

The slight bitterness of the endive in this salad works well with the sweetness of the pears and the strong mustard dressing.

Serves 6   Prep 10 mins

Ingredients

7oz (200g) baby spinach leaves

2 heads curly endive, core removed and leaves separated

2 firm, ripe pears, peeled and sliced

3 shallots, thinly sliced

For the dressing

1 tbsp honey

½ tbsp Dijon mustard

⅓ cup extra-virgin olive oil

2 tbsp red wine vinegar

salt and freshly ground black pepper

Method

1 To make the vinaigrette, place the honey, mustard, oil, and vinegar in a screw-top jar and shake well. Season to taste with salt and pepper. Alternatively, whisk the ingredients together in a bowl.

2 Place the spinach, endive, sliced pears, and shallots in a salad bowl. Drizzle with the vinaigrette, gently toss to coat, and serve.

Nutrition per serving

Energy	171cals (657kJ)
Carbohydrate	12g
of which sugar	10g
Fat	12g
of which saturated	2g
Sodium	0.1g
Fiber	5g

On the go

This salad is an easy way to improve your five-a-day intake. Double the portions given for a filling, portable lunch.

	Spinach
	Endive
	Shallots
	Pears
	Dressing

Mixed mushroom and orange salad

Raw mushrooms are marinated in a delicate mustard vinaigrette to create a refreshing and unique light salad. If you do not like the texture of raw mushrooms, fry them for a few minutes beforehand to soften them.

Serves 4   Prep 15 mins

Ingredients

9oz (250g) mixed mushrooms, sliced

pinch of red pepper flakes

1 bunch of scallions, sliced

1–2 oranges, depending on size, segmented (p12), and juice reserved

2 handfuls of spinach leaves

handful of basil leaves, shredded

For the dressing

⅓ cup extra-virgin olive oil

3 tbsp apple cider vinegar

pinch of sugar

1 tsp whole-grain mustard

salt and freshly ground black pepper

Nutrition per serving

Energy	215cals (861kJ)
Carbohydrate	11g
of which sugar	11g
Fat	17g
of which saturated	2.5g
Sodium	0.1g
Fiber	2.5g

Method

1 First, make the dressing. Pour the olive oil and vinegar in a small bowl, and whisk until combined. Add a little bit of the juice reserved from segmenting the oranges for the salad, along with the sugar and mustard. Season with salt and black pepper, whisk again, and taste. Add a little more of the orange juice, if needed. Let the dressing stand for a while, to develop the flavors

2 To make the salad, place the mushrooms in a large bowl. Add the pepper flakes, and drizzle with a little of the dressing. Toss to coat. Let stand for at least 10 minutes, then add the scallions and orange segments, and gently toss to combine.

3 When ready to serve, add the spinach and basil leaves, as well as more of the dressing. Taste, and season again, if needed. Serve immediately.

Butternut squash and avocado salad

Roasted squash is a nice late-year treat. Serve this salad warm for a fall meal, or eat it cold as an on-the-go lunch. This recipe calls for butternut squash, but you could also try pumpkin if it is in season.

Serves 4   Prep 15 mins   Cook 25 mins

Ingredients

salt and freshly ground black pepper

1 butternut squash, chopped into chunks

1 tbsp olive oil

1–2 tsp red pepper flakes

9oz (250g) arugula

9oz (250g) spinach leaves

2 ripe avocados, peeled, pitted, and sliced

2 tomatoes, skinned and finely chopped

1 tbsp flat-leaf parsley

For the dressing

3 tbsp olive oil

1 tbsp lemon juice

zest of ½ lemon

½ tsp mayonnaise

Method

1 Preheat the oven to 400°F (200°C). Meanwhile, put all the dressing ingredients in a small bowl and whisk to combine. Season to taste and set aside.

2 Put the butternut squash in a large roasting pan, drizzle with the olive oil, and mix well with your hands. Season, then sprinkle over the pepper flakes. Roast in the oven for 20–30 minutes or until soft and beginning to char. Remove from the oven and allow to cool slightly.

3 Put the arugula and spinach leaves into a large serving bowl and add the avocado pieces. Top with the squash and toss gently to combine, then scatter the chopped tomatoes on top. When ready to serve, whisk the dressing and drizzle it over the salad. Finish with a sprinkling of parsley.

Nutrition per serving	
Energy	345cals (1434kJ)
Carbohydrate	19g
of which sugar	11g
Fat	27g
of which saturated	5g
Sodium	0.3g
Fiber	8g

On the go

Let the squash cool completely on a piece of paper towel (to absorb any excess moisture) before layering this salad.

- Arugula and spinach
- Tomato
- Avocado
- Squash
- Dressing, herbs, and red pepper flakes

Bean thread noodle salad

This light, Asian-inspired meal is a vibrant and refreshing summer salad with crunchy raw vegetables. Finely slicing vegetables is a test of good knife work, but you could also use a mandoline or spiralizer to do the job for you.

Serves 4   Prep 20 mins

Ingredients

7oz (200g) dried Chinese bean thread noodles or thin rice noodles

1 large carrot, shaved using a vegetable peeler

1 × 4in (10cm) cucumber, halved lengthwise, seeded, and thinly sliced diagonally

4 scallions, white parts only, thinly sliced diagonally

1 mango, not too ripe, finely julienned

handful of mint leaves, roughly chopped

handful of cilantro, roughly chopped

For the dressing

juice of 2 limes

2 tbsp white wine vinegar or rice wine vinegar

1 tsp sugar

pinch of salt

Method

1 Put the noodles in a large bowl and cover with boiling water. Stir and separate the strands with a fork, then leave for 4 minutes, or according to the package instructions, until they are soft but still have a bite to them. Stir once or twice during cooking to keep the strands loose. Drain and refresh under cold water, then drain thoroughly.

2 Meanwhile, assemble the rest of the salad ingredients in a bowl, leaving out a few herbs to serve. Pat the noodles completely dry with paper towels, then add them to the bowl.

3 Whisk together the dressing ingredients and toss with the salad to coat. Serve, scattered with the reserved herbs.

Nutrition per serving	
Energy	228cals (957kJ)
Carbohydrate	48g
of which sugar	10g
Fat	0.5g
of which saturated	0.1g
Sodium	0.5g
Fiber	3g

On the go

Dry the noodles completely before adding them to your container, so they don't end up too soggy.

- Scallions
- Noodles
- Mango and cucumber
- Carrot
- Dressing and herbs

Edamame and snow pea salad

Edamame beans (also known as soybeans) are usually bought frozen and are useful to have in reserve in the freezer. Here, they are dished up in a bright salad and drizzled with a tangy sweet chili dressing.

Serves 4   Prep 10 mins   Cook 5 mins

Ingredients

7oz (200g) frozen edamame beans (soybeans)

7oz (200g) green beans, trimmed

7oz (200g) snow peas

8oz (225g) cherry tomatoes, sliced in half

3 scallions, finely chopped

2 tbsp chopped cilantro

For the dressing

3 tbsp rice wine vinegar

3 tbsp sweet chili sauce

Method

1 Place the edamame beans in a large pot of boiling water for 3 minutes. Add the green beans and snow peas, and cook for 2 minutes. Drain, refresh under cold running water and then drain again well.

2 Place the cooked beans and peas in a large bowl. Add the cherry tomatoes, scallions, and cilantro.

3 Whisk together the vinegar and sweet chili sauce. Drizzle it over the vegetables, toss well, and serve.

Nutrition per serving

Energy	142cals (595kJ)
Carbohydrate	18g
of which sugar	11g
Fat	4g
of which saturated	0.7g
Sodium	0.3g
Fiber	5g

On the go

To preserve the wonderful crunch of this salad, you can keep the sweet chili dressing separate if you wish.

- Cilantro
- Scallions
- Cherry tomatoes
- Beans and peas
- Sweet chili dressing

Marinated cucumber and dill salad

This beautifully simple Scandinavian dish is an elegant accompaniment to a piece of grilled or cold poached salmon. The cooling cucumber adds color as well as crunch.

Serves 4   Prep 10 mins, plus draining and chilling

Ingredients

2 cucumbers, thinly sliced using a mandoline

2 tbsp coarse sea salt

2 tbsp sugar

¼ cup rice wine vinegar or white wine vinegar

freshly ground black pepper

handful of dill, finely chopped

juice of ½ lemon (optional)

Method

1 Put the sliced cucumbers in a colander and sprinkle over the sea salt. Place a slightly smaller bowl on top of the cucumber and weigh down with weights, or a few unopened cans of food. Leave the colander over a sink for 1 hour to allow the cucumbers to lose any excess water.

2 Remove the weights, wrap the cucumber carefully in a clean kitchen towel, and squeeze out the excess water. Transfer to a bowl, cover, and refrigerate for at least 1 hour, until completely chilled.

3 Meanwhile, put 2 tablespoons of boiling water into a bowl and stir in the sugar to dissolve. Then add the vinegar, a generous amount of black pepper, and the dill, and place the bowl in the fridge to cool. Once the dressing and cucumber are completely cold, mix the two together. Adjust the seasoning to taste before serving. If using rice wine vinegar, add the lemon juice to balance out the flavor.

Nutrition per serving

Energy	61cals (259kJ)
Carbohydrate	10g
of which sugar	10g
Fat	0g
of which saturated	0g
Sodium	4.9g
Fiber	1.5g

Picnic potato and dill pickle salad

Tender new potatoes are bathed in a sauce of mayonnaise and herbs, as well as lots of crunchy celery and dill pickles, in this hard-to-beat potato salad. It is perfect for picnics or as a summery side dish.

Serves 14   Prep 10 mins   Cook 15 mins, plus cooling time

Ingredients

3lb (1.35kg) small new potatoes
1 red onion, finely chopped
4 sticks celery, finely chopped
½ cup dill pickle. finely
   chopped

For the dressing

¾ cup mayonnaise
¼ cup extra-virgin olive oil
2 tbsp whole-grain Dijon mustard
2 tbsp apple cider vinegar
2 tbsp dill, finely chopped
2 tbsp flat-leaf parsley, finely
   chopped
1 tsp hot sauce
salt and freshly ground
   black pepper

Method

1 In a pot with a tight-fitting lid, bring 2in (5cm) of water to a boil over medium-high heat. Place the new potatoes in a steamer basket, set in the pot, and steam for about 10 minutes or until tender and easily pierced with a fork. Transfer to a wide colander to drain and cool for 15 minutes.

2 Meanwhile, in a large bowl, whisk together the dressing ingredients until smooth and well combined. Transfer half of this dressing to a small bowl and set aside.

3 When the potatoes are cool enough to handle, cut into halves or quarters. Fold the red onion, celery, and dill pickle into the sauce in the large bowl, then gently fold in the potatoes. Refrigerate along with the reserved dressing for 1 hour or until chilled.

4 Fold in the reserved dressing and serve. This potato salad will keep in the fridge for up to 3 days.

Nutrition per serving

Energy	202cals (831kJ)
Carbohydrate	15.5g
of which sugar	2g
Fat	14g
of which saturated	2g
Sodium	0.6g
Fiber	2g

On the go

Make a large batch of this salad to enjoy over several days, or a smaller portion for a one-off lunchtime treat.

Dill pickle
Celery and red onion
Potatoes
Dressing

Warm potato salad
with mustard vinaigrette

The taste of these potatoes shouts loud as they are dressed quite simply, with plenty of shallots and a whole-grain mustard dressing, spooned over a bed of tender baby salad leaves.

Serves 4   Prep 5 mins   Cook 10 mins

Ingredients

1lb (450g) small fingerling potatoes, halved lengthwise

14oz (400g) salad leaves

For the dressing

1 shallot, halved and very thinly sliced

2 tbsp whole-grain Dijon mustard

¼ cup sherry vinegar

1 tsp sea salt

½ cup extra-virgin olive oil

2 tbsp chervil, finely chopped

2 tbsp chives, finely chopped

2 tbsp flat-leaf parsley, finely chopped

½ tsp freshly ground black pepper

Method

1 In a pot with a tight-fitting lid, bring 2in (5cm) of water to a boil over medium-high heat. Place the potatoes in a steamer basket, set in the pot, and steam for about 8–10 minutes or until tender and easily pierced with a fork. Transfer the potatoes to a large bowl.

2 While the potatoes are steaming, in a small bowl, whisk together the shallots, mustard, vinegar, and salt. Slowly whisk in the extra-virgin olive oil in a thin stream, then whisk in the chopped herbs and black pepper.

3 Reserve ¼ cup of dressing, and toss the potatoes with the remainder of the dressing.

4 Divide the salad leaves between 4 chilled individual plates, spoon one-quarter of the potato salad over the leaves, and drizzle each serving with 1 tablespoon of the reserved dressing. Serve immediately.

Nutrition per serving

Energy	309cals (1261kJ)
Carbohydrate	19g
of which sugar	3.5g
Fat	23g
of which saturated	3g
Sodium	1.6g
Fiber	4g

Dressings and sauces

Even the most perfect salad can be improved by a dressing, whether you choose a delicate drizzle of vinaigrette or a dollop of pesto. The dedicated dressing recipes in this chapter are worthy of any salad—try them and see for yourself.

Dressing basics

Vinaigrette dressings are very easy to make, and add a welcome tartness to any salad. Why not try one of the many vinaigrettes found throughout this book using the steps below—or even invent your own?

Building a dressing

Standard vinaigrette dressings tend to follow a simple ratio of components: 3 parts oil (or oil-based ingredient) to 1 part acid (such as vinegar or citrus juice). In addition, seasonings and flavorings can be added; usually about ½ part of each will provide a balanced taste. Provided you keep to these ratios and choose suitable ingredients (see Dressing components, right), you can whip up your own unique vinaigrette inventions by following the steps below.

 **3 parts oil**

 **1 part acid**

 **½ part flavoring**

½ part seasoning

Basic vinaigrette

1 Measure out your ingredients—no matter the quantity, you generally need 3 parts oil to 1 part acid.

2 Combine the oil and acid together with any other flavoring ingredients you wish to use.

3 Whisk thoroughly to emulsify (combine) the ingredients. Add any flavorings or seasonings you wish to use and whisk again.

Dressing components

Be inspired by some of the vinaigrette ingredients suggested below, and build your own ideal vinaigrette dressing for your favorite salad.

3 parts oil

Add 3 parts of any of the following:

- olive oil
- extra-virgin olive oil
- sunflower oil
- hazelnut oil
- peanut oil
- mayonnaise
- Greek-style yogurt
- sour cream

1 part acid

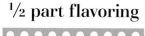

Add 1 part of any of the following:

- white wine vinegar
- red wine vinegar
- rice wine vinegar
- balsamic vinegar
- apple cider vinegar
- fruit vinegar
- lemon juice
- lime juice

½ part flavoring

Add ½ part of any of the following:

- mustard
- honey
- soy sauce
- sweet chili sauce
- sesame oil
- miso paste
- pesto
- citrus zest, grated
- garlic, crushed
- berries, crushed
- olives, diced
- fresh chiles, diced
- onions, diced
- anchovies, chopped
- Parmesan cheese, grated
- blue cheese, crumbled

½ part seasoning

Add to taste:

- salt and pepper
- sugar
- red pepper flakes
- herbs (fresh or dried)
- dried spices
- curry powder

Dressing tips

Sesame oil has a rich, nutty taste that works better as a flavoring than as a base. Try pairing it with **sunflower** or **peanut oil**.

Avoid **malt vinegar**, which is too overpowering for most dressings.

Some of the salads in this book do not feature a specific dressing recipe. Instead, the components are often tossed in a simple oil-acid mixture of **extra-virgin olive oil** and **lemon juice**. Omit these ingredients if you want to add your own dressing to the salad instead.

Storing dressings

If not being used immediately, dressings should be **covered and stored in the fridge**. They can be kept for **up to 3 days**.

Remember to **remove the dressing from the fridge at least 1 hour before using**, to bring it back to room temperature.

Vinaigrette dressings often **split** during storage, with the oil rising to the surface. This is natural—simply **whisk the mixture again** to re-emulsify the vinaigrette, then pour it over the salad as usual. You can also store vinaigrette in **any container with a vinegar-proof lid**. Simply shake the container to re-emulsify the contents before serving.

Chile and ginger vinaigrette

This Asian-inspired dressing has a complex flavor; prepare a few hours ahead to allow the ginger and lemongrass to fully infuse. It is an excellent choice for noodle salads, such as the Mixed seafood salad (p38).

Serves 10   Prep 5 mins, plus standing

Ingredients

2 tbsp white wine vinegar

juice of ½ lime

pinch of sugar

⅓ cup extra-virgin olive oil

1 red chile, seeded and finely diced

1 x 1in (2.5cm) piece of fresh ginger, peeled and grated

2 garlic cloves, peeled and grated

2 lemongrass stalks, ends trimmed and outer leaves discarded

salt and freshly ground black pepper

Method

1 Combine the vinegar, lime juice, and sugar in a small bowl. Add the oil in a steady stream and whisk until the mixture has emulsified.

2 Add the remaining ingredients, season to taste with salt and black pepper, and whisk to combine. Set aside for a few hours to develop the flavors.

3 Remove the lemongrass stalks just before serving. If the ingredients have separated, whisk again to re-emulsify.

Nutrition per serving

Energy	89cals (361kJ)
Carbohydrate	0.6g
of which sugar	0.5g
Fat	9.5g
of which saturated	1.4g
Sodium	0.1g
Fiber	0g

Tomato and paprika vinaigrette

The rich flavors and gentle heat of this chunky tomato vinaigrette makes it an ideal dressing for drizzling over a pasta or rice salad—try it with the Tomato and farfalle pasta salad (p152).

Serves 6   Prep 10 mins   Cook 10 mins

Ingredients

3 ripe tomatoes, peeled (see p9)

3 tbsp extra-virgin olive oil

2 garlic cloves, crushed

¼ tsp hot paprika

1 tbsp finely chopped basil

1 tbsp finely chopped
  flat-leaf parsley

1 tbsp sherry vinegar

salt and freshly ground
  black pepper

Method

1 Halve the peeled tomatoes, then scoop out and discard the seeds. Remove the tomato core, dice the flesh, and set aside.

2 Put the olive oil in a pan over very low heat, and add the garlic and paprika. Stir for 3–4 minutes. Add half the basil and parsley, and stir for 1 minute. Add the tomatoes and stir gently for 2–3 minutes, until hot.

3 Remove from the heat. Stir in the remaining basil and parsley, and then the sherry vinegar. Season with salt and black pepper to taste, and serve while still warm.

Nutrition per serving

Energy	59cals (240kJ)
Carbohydrate	1.5g
of which sugar	1.5g
Fat	5.5g
of which saturated	0.8g
Sodium	trace
Fiber	0.6g

Apple cider vinaigrette

Whisk together this simple, tangy vinaigrette dressing in minutes to give your salads a flavor-packed punch. Nonalcoholic apple cider vinegar is available in health food stores and larger supermarkets.

Serves 8   Prep 10 mins

Ingredients

1 small shallot, finely minced

1 tbsp finely chopped fresh herbs, such as chives, tarragon, or parsley

¼ cup apple cider vinegar

salt and freshly ground black pepper

½ tbsp Dijon mustard

¼ cup extra-virgin olive oil

Method

1 In a small bowl, whisk together the shallot, herbs, apple cider vinegar, salt, and Dijon mustard.

2 Slowly whisk in the extra-virgin olive oil, a few drops at a time, until the dressing is smooth and all the oil has been incorporated.

3 Season with black pepper and use immediately, or refrigerate in a tightly sealed container for up to 3 days.

Nutrition per serving

Energy	52cals (218kJ)
Carbohydrate	0g
of which sugar	0g
Fat	5.5g
of which saturated	0.8g
Sodium	0.2g
Fiber	0g

Classic blue cheese vinaigrette

This rich dressing is a little thicker than most vinaigrettes, and should be used sparingly. It is traditionally drizzled over crisp leaf salads, such as the Endive salad with spinach and pears (p163).

Serves 8   Prep 10 mins

Ingredients

1 tbsp white wine or apple cider vinegar

1½ tsp lemon juice

1 tsp mayonnaise

3 tbsp extra-virgin olive oil

¼ cup gorgonzola cheese, crumbled

salt and freshly ground black pepper

Method

1 Combine the vinegar and lemon juice in a bowl. Add the mayonnaise and oil to a separate bowl, then pour in the vinegar-lemon mixture, whisking constantly, until the dressing has emulsified.

2 Add the cheese to the bowl, and whisk again until smooth. Season to taste with salt and black pepper. Serve immediately.

Nutrition per serving

Energy	88cals (366kJ)
Carbohydrate	0.1g
of which sugar	0.1g
Fat	9.1g
of which saturated	2.5g
Sodium	0.1g
Fiber	0g

Lemongrass and chile salsa

This is a fantastically fresh, spicy salsa. The combination of Asian flavors and vibrant colors will transform meat- and fish-based salads, such as the Thai-spiced lamb salad (p64).

Serves 6   Prep 20 mins, plus chilling

Ingredients

2 stalks of lemongrass, outer leaves discarded

2 heaping tbsp chopped Thai or Italian basil, plus 6 whole leaves to finish

1 tsp grated ginger

1 red chile, seeded and finely chopped

1 tbsp honey or 1 tbsp sugar

3 tbsp soy sauce

2 tsp Thai fish sauce

⅓ cup lime juice

Method

1 Slice off the tops of the lemongrass stalks and discard them. Bash down on the bulb ends with the flat side of a large knife or pound using a kitchen mallet. Chop very finely and place in a bowl.

2 Add the basil, ginger, and chile. Pour in the honey, soy sauce, Thai fish sauce, and lime juice, and stir well. Cover and chill for at least 1 hour to help develop the flavors.

3 Stir in the whole basil leaves just before serving. The salsa can be stored in the fridge for up to 2 days.

Nutrition per serving

Energy	17cals (76kJ)
Carbohydrate	4g
of which sugar	4g
Fat	0g
of which saturated	0g
Sodium	1.5g
Fiber	0g

Dill and watercress salsa with capers

This fresh and herbed salsa makes a perfect partner for salads containing fish or meat. Try tossing it into the Tuna, artichoke, and pasta salad (p20) to give the dish a citrus tang.

Serves 6   Prep 15 mins, plus chilling

Ingredients

2 tbsp chopped dill weed

1¾oz (50g) picked watercress leaves, chopped

9 baby cherry tomatoes, halved

1 heaping tbsp capers, drained

juice and finely grated zest of ½ lemon

sea salt and freshly ground black pepper

3 tbsp extra-virgin olive oil

Method

1 Put the dill and watercress in a bowl. Gently squeeze the halved cherry tomatoes to discard some of the seeds, then slice into quarters, and add to the bowl.

2 Chop the capers and stir into the tomato mixture, along with the lemon juice and zest. Stir, season with salt and pepper, and drizzle with olive oil.

3 Chill the salsa for at least 30 minutes to allow the flavors to blend. Stir again before serving.

Nutrition per serving

Energy	59cals (241kJ)
Carbohydrate	1g
of which sugar	1g
Fat	6g
of which saturated	0.8g
Sodium	trace
Fiber	0.5g

Cilantro and walnut pesto

Try this tasty alternative to the more common basil and pine nut pesto, found in the Caprese farro salad (p81). It can be used in the same way: stir it into pasta dishes, or use it top goat cheese rounds (p79 and p88).

Serves 12   Prep 10 mins

Ingredients

small bunch of cilantro, approx. 1oz (30g), stems removed

1 large garlic clove, lightly crushed

¼ cup walnut pieces

sea salt and freshly ground black pepper

¼ cup freshly grated Parmesan cheese

⅓ cup extra-virgin olive oil

Method

1 Put the cilantro leaves in a blender or food processor with the garlic, walnuts, a generous amount of black pepper, a pinch of salt, the cheese, and 1 tablespoon of the oil. Blend the ingredients, stopping to scrape down the sides of the bowl as necessary.

2 With the machine still running, gradually add 3 tablespoons of the oil, a little at a time, until you have a glistening, thin paste.

3 Spoon the pesto into a sterilized jar, top with the remaining 1 tablespoon of oil to prevent air getting in, screw on the lid, and store in the fridge.

This pesto will keep, refrigerated, for 2 weeks. If you don't use all the pesto at once, cover the remainder with 1 tablespoon of olive oil and rescrew the lid.

Nutrition per serving

Energy	70cals (288kJ)
Carbohydrate	0g
of which sugar	0g
Fat	7g
of which saturated	1.5g
Sodium	trace
Fiber	0g

Traditional French garlic aïoli

Typically served alongside raw or lightly steamed baby vegetables and hard-boiled eggs, this rich sauce will make a wonderful addition to any French dish, such as the Bistro salad with frisée lettuce (p58).

Serves 10   Prep 20 mins, plus resting

Ingredients

2 large garlic cloves, smashed and peeled

sea salt and freshly ground black pepper

1 large egg yolk

1 cup light olive oil

Method

1 Using a mortar and pestle, pound the garlic with a small pinch of salt. Add the egg yolk and season with pepper. Beat for 1 minute, then let rest for 5 minutes.

2 Beat in the oil, a few drops at a time, to make the mayonnaise. Once the sauce has emulsified, pour in the olive oil in a thin trickle, beating continually with the pestle in the same direction. The sauce is ready once it has a very thick texture and the pestle almost stands up by itself in the bowl.

3 Cover and refrigerate for up to 24 hours, until ready to use.

Nutrition per serving

Energy	69cals (284kJ)
Carbohydrate	0g
of which sugar	0g
Fat	7.5g
of which saturated	1.1g
Sodium	0.2g
Fiber	0g

Hummus

Rich, creamy, nutritious hummus is filled with the flavors of garlic, lemon, and tahini (sesame seed paste). Serve it with Fattoush (p156), scooping up the dip with the toasted flatbread.

Serves 6   Prep 10 mins, plus overnight soaking   Cook 1 hr 30 mins

Ingredients

1 × 14oz (400g) can chickpeas, drained

2 tsp sea salt

2 tbsp lemon juice

2 cloves garlic, smashed and chopped

¼ cup tahini

½ cup plus 2 tbsp extra-virgin olive oil

1 tsp ground sumac

Method

1 Pour the chickpeas into a colander. Rinse under running water, then drain.

2 Place the drained chickpeas in a large saucepan, reserving a few for garnish if wished. Add enough water to cover by 1in (2.5cm), and bring to a boil. Reduce the heat to low so that the chickpeas bubble at a gentle simmer, and cook for 30 minutes.

3 Add salt, and cook for 1 more hour, or until the chickpeas are soft and tender.

4 Drain the chickpeas thoroughly, reserving ¾ cup of the cooking liquid.

5 Place the warm chickpeas in a food processor fitted with a metal blade. Add the lemon juice, garlic, and tahini, and pulse to combine. With the machine running, slowly drizzle in ½ cup extra-virgin olive oil, followed by the reserved cooking liquid.

6 Spread the hummus in a shallow bowl, and make a well in the center. Pour the remaining 2 tablespoons of extra-virgin olive oil into the well. Serve immediately, garnished with sumac and the reserved chickpeas, or refrigerate in a sealed container for up to 5 days.

Nutrition per serving

Energy	557cals (2202kJ)
Carbohydrate	38g
of which sugar	2g
Fat	33.5g
of which saturated	4.5g
Sodium	2g
Fiber	13g

At-a-glance dressings, sauces, and dips

Reinvent any of the salad recipes in this book by mixing it up with an entirely different dressing. This reference page will help you find your favorites.

Lime dressing

Dressings, vinaigrettes, and pestos:

Anchovy dressing 38

Antipasto dressing 54

Apple cider vinaigrette 178

Blue cheese dressing 84

Caesar dressing 47

Chile and ginger vinaigrette 176

Chive dressing 87

Cilantro and walnut pesto 182

Cilantro-orange vinaigrette 128

Classic blue cheese vinaigrette 179

Crunchy soy vinaigrette 146

Curried vingaigrette 122

Ginger vinaigrette 120

Grainy mustard vinaigrette 171

Herb vinaigrette 74

Horseradish dressing 62

Italian balsamic dressing 22

Lemon-mayonnaise dressing 165

Lime dressing 64

Mustard-dill vinaigrette 75

Orange dressing 155

Peanut dressing 49

Pomegranate molasses 106

Raspberry dressing 29

Red wine vinaigrette 154

Romesco dressing 142

Shepherd's dressing 159

Tahini dressing 131

Thai chile dressing 148

Tomato and paprika vinaigrette 177

Traditional pesto 81

Vietnamese lemongrass dressing 60

Walnut oil dressing 136

White wine vinaigrette 40

Sauces, salsas, and dips:

Cacık 104

Curried yogurt 53

Dill and watercress salsa with capers 181

Dill relish 26

Hummus 184

Lemongrass and chile salsa 180

Olive salsa 63

Papaya salsa 52

Spiced yogurt 27

Traditional French garlic aïoli 183

Watercress mayonnaise 70

Pesto

Salads index

A

anchovies
Mixed seafood salad 38–39
Niçoise-style salad 24–25
Antipasto salad 54–55

apples
Celery and green apple salad 84
Waldorf salad 158

apricots
Couscous with pine nuts and almonds 94
Jeweled couscous and apricot salad 92–93
Arabic salad 159

artichokes
Antipasto salad 54–55
Artichoke salad with lemon juice 149
Chickpea, red rice, and artichoke salad 128–29
Grilled vegetable and spinach bowl 138
Lentil, artichoke, and red pepper salad 118–19
Tuna, artichoke, and pasta salad 20–21

asparagus
Chicken, radicchio, and asparagus salad 44–45
Grilled vegetable and spinach bowl 138
Spring rice salad with smoked salmon 30

avocado 14
Avocado, cilantro, and lime tabbouleh 102–03
Butternut squash and avocado salad 165
Chile crab and avocado salad 41
Mexican quinoa and kidney bean salad 114–15
Smoked trout salad with pickled cucumber 23

B

barley
Grilled broccoli rabe 142
Lentils and barley with sweet potato 117

Nutty pearl barley and lentil salad 124–25
Pearl barley, squash, and tomato salad 123

beans
Antipasto salad 54–55
Chicken with adzuki beans and parsley 48
Chile shrimp with cilantro and lime 32–33
Edamame and snow pea salad 168
Fava bean and feta panzanella bowl 68–69
Flageolet beans with smoked cheese 121
Gingered fava beans with lentils 120
Goat cheese and beans 86–87
Mexican quinoa and kidney bean salad 114–15
Niçoise-style salad 24–25
Quinoa and mango with toasted coconut 110–11
Salmon salad 28–29
Tuna, artichoke, and pasta salad 20–21

beef
Green papaya, beef, and noodle salad 60–61
Nutty bresaola salad 62
Pastrami and arugula salad 63

beets
Grated carrot and beet salad 146
Herbed mackerel salad 18–19
Nutty goat cheese and beet salad 89
Roasted beet and orange salad 140–41
Smoked trout and endive 26
Bistro salad with frisée lettuce 58

blue cheese
Celery and green apple salad 84
Gorgonzola and ciabatta salad 83
Wheat berries and roasted squash with blue cheese 85

broccoli
Grilled broccoli rabe 142

bulgur wheat
Avocado, cilantro, and lime tabbouleh 102–03

Bulgur, eggplant, and pomegranate seed salad 99
Bulgur wheat with mixed peppers and goat cheese 98
Bulgur wheat with shrimp and okra 34–35
Chickpea, bulgur, and cranberry salad 107
Herb tabbouleh 106
Rustic tabbouleh 100–01
Tabbouleh with cacık 104–05
Triple-grain herbed salad bowl 130

butternut squash
Butternut squash and avocado salad 165
Freekeh sweet and spicy warm salad 108–09
Pearl barley, squash, and tomato salad 123
Wheat berries and roasted squash with blue cheese 85

C

cabbage
Curried rice and radish salad 126
Shredded carrot and cabbage with nuts 148

carrots
Bean thread noodle salad 166–67
Grated carrot and beet salad 146
Rainbow wheat berry and feta salad 72–73
Shredded carrot and cabbage with nuts 148
Spicy chicken salad with raw vegetables 50–51

cauliflower
Neapolitan Christmas salad 144–45

celery
Celery and green apple salad 84
Picnic potato and dill pickle salad 170
Spring rice salad with smoked salmon 30
Waldorf salad 158
Celery root and mustard remoulade 139

DK UK

Editorial Assistant Amy Slack
Design Assistant Philippa Nash
Jacket Assistant Steven Marsden
Pre-Production Producer Catherine Williams
Producer Nancy-Jane Maun
Creative Technical Support Sonia Charbonnier
Managing Editor Stephanie Farrow
Managing Art Editor Christine Keilty
US Editor Kayla Dugger

DK INDIA

Editor Sugandh Juneja
Project Editor Arani Sinha
Art Editor Sourabh Challariya
Pre-Production Manager Sunil Sharma
Senior DTP Designer Pushpak Tyagi
DTP Designer Umesh Rawat
Managing Editor Soma B. Chowdhury
Managing Art Editor Navidita Thapa

First American Edition, 2017
Published in the United States by DK Publishing
345 Hudson Street, New York, New York 10014

Copyright © 2017 Dorling Kindersley Limited
DK, a Division of Penguin Random House LLC
17 18 19 20 21 10 9 8 7 6 5 4 3 2 1
001–304621–June/2017

Published in Great Britain by Dorling Kindersley Limited.

A catalog record for this book is available from
the Library of Congress.
ISBN 978-1-4654-6199-5

DK books are available at special discounts when purchased
in bulk for sales promotions, premiums, fund-raising, or educational
use. For details, contact: DK Publishing Special Markets, 345 Hudson
Street, New York, New York 10014 SpecialSales@dk.com

Printed and bound in China

All images © Dorling Kindersley Limited
For further information see: www.dkimages.com

A WORLD OF IDEAS:
SEE ALL THERE IS TO KNOW

www.dk.com

Acknowledgments

We would like to thank Fiona Hunter for nutritional analysis,
Margaret McIntyre for supplying the index, and Alice Horne
for editorial assistance.

Content in this book has previously appeared in:
The Cooking Book (2008), *Grown in Britain Cookbook* (2008),
Quick Cook (2009), *The Cook's Herb Garden* (2010), *Cook Step by
Step* (2010), *Diabetes Cooking Book* (2010), *The Preserving Book*
(2010), *Allotment Cookbook* (2011), *Cooking Through the Year*
(2012), *Gluten Free Cookbook* (2012), *Family Cookbook* (2013),
Neal's Yard Remedies Healing Foods (2013), *The Meat Book*
(2014), *Mediterranean Cookbook* (2014), *Grains as Mains* (2015),
Plant-Based Cookbook (2016)